PRAISE FOR *THE STUDENT DEBT CRISIS*

"Student debt is a crisis that unites large swaths of the American public across axes of race, class, and gender. Jamal Watson's brilliant book *The Student Debt Crisis* is both timely and necessary. One of America's leading public intellectuals delivers an analytical history of this pressing issue while offering an impassioned plea for relief of debt that crushes the future of millions of citizens. This compelling and cogent moral argument for national assistance to vulnerable members of our society should be read by all—but especially by politicians who hold the purse strings and public-policy makers who put their visions into action."

—**Michael Eric Dyson**, University Distinguished
Professor of African American and Diaspora
Studies, Vanderbilt University

"If you're looking for a compelling and comprehensive book on student loan debt, then look no further. Watson has written a groundbreaking book, sharing policy, data, and real stories, that persuasively calls for action, especially around racial justice. He calls for an end to blaming the victim and makes the case that college is one American dream that students should not be penalized with extraordinary fiscal debt for pursuing. Watson offers moral, practical, doable recommendations to support and honor those seeking a college degree. A must-read from beginning to end."

—**Donna Y. Ford**, Distinguished Professor of Education
and Human Ecology, The Ohio State University

"Jamal Watson's *The Student Debt Crisis* is both a brilliant call to arms regarding one of the pressing civil rights issues of the era and an insightful and urgent moral plea to reimagine the possibility and promise of American democracy. An excellent and invigorating read."

—**Dr. Peniel E. Joseph**, author of *The Sword and the Shield* and *The Third Reconstruction*, among other books, and founding director of the Center for the Study of Race and Democracy at the University of Texas at Austin

"Jamal Watson has written a superb and courageous book on a crucial yet overlooked issue: student debt. His visionary scholarship continues to matter!"

—**Cornel West**, author of *Race Matters* and the Dietrich Bonhoeffer Professor of Philosophy & Christian Practice at Union Theological Seminary

THE STUDENT DEBT CRISIS

The Student Debt Crisis

Foreword by
Al Sharpton

America's Moral Urgency

Jamal Watson
Diverse: Issues In Higher Education

Broadleaf Books
Minneapolis

THE STUDENT DEBT CRISIS
America's Moral Urgency

31 30 29 28 27 26 25   1 2 3 4 5 6 7 8 9

Library of Congress Control Number: 2024951604 (print)

Cover design: Broadleaf Books

Print ISBN: 978-1-5064-9516-3
eBook ISBN: 978-1-5064-9517-0

Printed in India.

This book is dedicated to the memory of the late Dr. William E. Cox (1942–2022), the cofounder of *Diverse: Issues In Higher Education*.

This book is also dedicated to my beloved late mother, Carolyn Marie Watson. Thank you for investing so much in me.

CONTENTS

CONTENTS

FOREWORD

by Reverend Al Sharpton

Let me be clear: The struggle for economic justice in America has never been a straight line. It's been a winding road through the mountains of resistance, through the valleys of setbacks, and, yes, even through the storms of political upheaval. Today, we find ourselves at another crossroads in our fight for educational equity and economic freedom for our young people.

Let me take you back to a moment that opened my eyes to this crisis. I was speaking at a rally in Detroit—must have been about ten years ago—when a young sister came up to me, tears streaming down her face. She was a nurse, first in her family to graduate from college, working two jobs, and still couldn't keep up with her student loan payments. Here was somebody who had done everything right—everything the system told her to do—and she was drowning in debt deeper than the Atlantic Ocean.

That sister in Detroit? She's not alone. I've met thousands like her across this nation. The straight-A student in Atlanta working as a barista because she can't afford to take an entry-level job in her field. The young brother in Oakland who had to move back in with his mama because his student loan payments eat up half his teaching salary. The single mother in the Bronx who tells me her kids might not go to college because she's still paying off her own student loans. These are not just stories. These are the faces of what I call the new economic segregation: student loan debt.

We're talking about 1.7 trillion dollars of dreams deferred, of futures mortgaged, of young people who did exactly what society told them to do—get an education—only to find themselves shackled by financial chains that would make the predatory lenders of yesteryear blush. And let me break it down for you: this crisis hits our Black and Brown communities the hardest. The average Black student borrower owes 95 percent of their original loan amount after twenty years of payments. Twenty years! That's not a debt—that's a life sentence.

Now, let me tell you something about Donald Trump—and I've known Trump a long time, from our days in New York. His reelection means we've got to shift our strategy. If you're waiting on the White House to feel your pain, you might as well be waiting on snow in the Sahara Desert. But let me tell you what history has taught us: When the front door is closed, we've always found another way in.

I remember when they said we couldn't desegregate the lunch counters. I remember when they said we couldn't pass the Voting Rights Act. I remember when they said we couldn't elect a Black president. But we did all that and more. Why? Because we understood something fundamental about power in America—it doesn't just flow from the top down, it flows from the bottom up.

That's why we need what I call a three-pronged attack:

1. *State-level legislation to protect borrowers:* We need to push every state legislature to pass their own Student Borrower

Bill of Rights. We need interest rate caps, strict oversight of loan servicers, and real penalties for predatory practices. If Washington won't protect our young people, then Albany and Sacramento and Atlanta will have to do it.

2. *Corporate accountability:* We need to make these institutions that have profited off our children's futures answer to the community. These colleges sitting on billion-dollar endowments while their graduates drown in debt? We're coming for you. These loan servicers making millions while "losing" paperwork and misleading borrowers? Your day of reckoning is coming.

3. *Mass mobilization:* This needs to happen not just in the streets but also in the voting booths, in the state houses, and, yes, in the boardrooms. We need a movement that brings together students and parents, workers and teachers, faith leaders and community organizers. We need what Dr. Martin Luther King Jr. called "the fierce urgency of now."

Some folks say, "But Reverend Al, what about personal responsibility?" Let me tell you something about responsibility. It's not responsible to create a system where the cost of education has risen over 180 percent in the last forty years, while wages have stayed flatter than yesterday's soda. It's not responsible to tell our young people that their only path to success is through college, then turn that path into a toll road with no exits.

And let me tell you about another kind of responsibility—the responsibility we have to each other. I'm reminded of something my mother used to tell me when I was coming up in Brownsville, Brooklyn. She'd say, "Al, when you make it up the ladder, you don't pull the ladder up behind you—you reach back and help somebody else up." That's what this fight is about.

This crisis isn't just about numbers on a spreadsheet. It's about the young couple in Chicago who can't buy a home because of their student debt. It's about the brilliant mind in Memphis who wanted to be a teacher but had to take a corporate job to pay off their loans. It's about the entrepreneur in Milwaukee who can't start a business because no bank will give them a loan while they're carrying so much student debt.

We need to understand something fundamental: This is a civil rights issue. When we talk about student debt, we're talking about the right to education, the right to economic opportunity, the right to pursue the American dream. And just like the civil rights movement of the 1960s, this fight will require all of us.

Here's what gives me hope: I see a new generation rising up. They understand something powerful: Their debt is not their fault, but their fight is their responsibility. I see young people organizing on campus, in their communities, on social media. They're not asking for permission to demand change—they're creating change.

This book you're holding isn't just about student debt, though Dr. Jamal Watson's analysis of the crisis is sharp as a razor. What he's done here is connect the dots between yesterday's struggles and today's fights. His chapter on Adam Clayton Powell's battles in Congress particularly moved me. You see, Powell understood, just as Watson helps us understand today, that the fight for educational equity isn't just about getting our people into the schoolhouse—it's about making sure they don't come out in financial chains.

Let me tell you what victory looks like: It looks like a future where education is a ladder up, not an anchor weighing you down. It looks like young people starting businesses, buying homes, raising families—without the shadow of debt hanging over their heads. It looks like an America living up to its promise of opportunity for all.

We've got work to do, family. The election didn't go our way, but we've been here before. When they close the front door, we've always found another way in. When they tell us to wait, we've always known how to march. And when they say it can't be done, we've always known how to prove them wrong.

The movement for student debt relief isn't dead. It's just moving to new battlegrounds. And if there's one thing I've learned in all my years of fighting for justice, it's that the power of the people is greater than the people in power.

Remember something: Every great movement in American history has faced setbacks. The abolitionists faced setbacks. The suffragettes faced setbacks. The civil rights movement faced setbacks. But they kept pushing, kept organizing, kept believing. And so must we.

To every young person reading this who's struggling under the weight of student debt: We see you. We hear you. And we're not giving up this fight. To every parent who's worried about how to send their kids to college without condemning them to a lifetime of debt: We're fighting for you too. To every graduate who's had to put their dreams on hold because of student loans: Your time is coming.

Keep marching. Keep fighting. Keep believing. And most importantly, keep organizing. Because in the words of the great Frederick Douglass, "Power concedes nothing without a demand." And we're about to make some demands that cannot be ignored.

Yours in Progress,
Reverend Al Sharpton
Founder and president, National Action Network
Host, *PoliticsNation*, MSNBC
Harlem, New York

INTRODUCTION

The student debt crisis is a racial justice issue, an economic issue, and a moral issue. Communities are grappling with increasing gas prices and food costs, and the more debt we cancel, the more people we will help.

NAACP President and CEO Derrick Johnson, delivering remarks at a 2022 press event organized by Massachusetts Senator Elizabeth Warren

By the summer of 2024, just a few months before Americans headed to the polls to cast their ballots in the presidential election, an astonishing 1 out of 10 student borrowers and more than 4.5 million Americans had already received some form of student loan forgiveness to the collective tune of nearly $167 billion. These individuals—primarily public servant workers like teachers, nurses, and law enforcement officers—were the beneficiaries of the Savings on a Valuable Education (SAVE) Plan. The popular income repayment program for federal student loan borrowers lowered student loan payments and forgave unpaid interest and low-balance loans after twenty or twenty-five years of continuous repayment.

One such beneficiary was Shauntee Russell. While policy debates and statistical analyses often dominate discussions about student loan forgiveness, it's the personal stories that truly illuminate the transformative impact of these programs. Russell's journey provides a compelling case study of how financial assistance programs can affect real lives, offering hope and opening new possibilities for those struggling under the heavy weight of educational debt. Her experience not only personalizes the statistics but also highlights the broader societal implications of addressing the student debt crisis head-on.

Russell embodies the resilience and determination of many Americans pursuing higher education while also balancing family responsibilities. At thirty-eight, she is a single mother of three children, juggling the demands of parenthood with a fast-paced career in nursing. Her story is set against the backdrop of Chicago, a city known for its diverse communities and complex socioeconomic landscape. As a Black woman in America, Russell has had a particularly significant journey. Black students are more likely to take on student debt and in larger amounts than their white peers, a disparity rooted in historical and ongoing racial wealth gaps. This makes her experience with student loan forgiveness not just a personal victory but also a small step toward addressing broader systemic inequities. In 2024, Russell took advantage of the SAVE program and received student loan forgiveness totaling $127,000. "The student loan forgiveness has made it so much easier to provide for my children," Russell told me,[1] highlighting the tangible impact of the financial assistance program on working families like hers. "I can't tell you how good it feels not to have to make that extra $632 payment each month. For the first time in my life, I can start saving and thinking about the future." For Russell, like many others, student loans weren't just numbers on a balance sheet. They represented the looming debt that affected every financial decision that she had to make, from grocery shopping to housing choices.

The wide-reaching scope of the SAVE Plan program was not only monumental and historic, but like so many of the other attempts that sought to provide remedies to our nation's ballooning and out-of-control student debt crisis, it would also face fierce opposition, mounting legal challenges, and an uncertainty about its future and longevity.

After the conservative-leaning US Supreme Court dealt a devastating blow in June 2023 to the Biden administration's plan to cancel $10,000 or $20,000 per student in federally owned debt, opponents of student debt relief set their sights on the SAVE Plan program. Their strategy appeared effective. A year after the Supreme Court handed down its decision, federal judges in Kansas and Missouri ruled against parts of the SAVE repayment plan, imposing an injunction and leaving borrowers confused and frustrated. Persis Yu, deputy executive director and managing counsel of the Student Borrower Protection Center, an advocacy group for student loan borrowers, described the situation as "unworkable chaos."[2]

While SAVE did not provide immediate, outright cancellation of student loans as some advocates had hoped for, it had gained traction with over eight million enrollees. The program aimed to help borrowers manage affordable monthly payments and avoid defaulting on their loans. SAVE was designed to halve undergraduate loan payments, prevent interest growth for borrowers making zero-dollar or low payments, and accelerate loan forgiveness for at-risk borrowers. Although it was not a panacea, SAVE was a key legislative victory that President Joe Biden and US Secretary of Education Miguel A. Cardona introduced to fulfill a 2020 campaign promise that had mobilized millions of voters to the polls. Upon SAVE's rollout in August 2023, Biden stated, "From day one of my Administration, I promised to fight to ensure higher education is a ticket to the middle class, not a barrier to opportunity."[3]

Indeed, conservative opposition to student debt cancellation has remained consistent over the years. National polls show that only about 7 percent of Republicans support complete student loan cancellation, while 26 percent favor partial cancellation and 57 percent oppose any form of cancellation. These figures contrast sharply with Democratic sentiment. Support among Democrats for canceling either some (45 percent) or all (26 percent) student debt has held steady.[4] Interestingly, most Americans (63 percent) favor making tuition at public colleges free, according to the Pew Research Center.[5] Support for free college tuition varies across racial demographics: 86 percent of Black adults, 82 percent of Latinx adults, and 69 percent of Asian American adults favor making college free for all Americans, compared to 53 percent of white adults. Age also plays a role, with 73 percent of adults under thirty supporting free college tuition while only 51 percent of those sixty-five and older do.

Despite attempts by the Republicans on Capitol Hill to block varying debt discharge initiatives, millions of Americans still experienced substantial relief between 2001 and 2024. By June 2024, the Biden administration had pledged an additional $7.7 billion in student loan debt relief for another 160,500 borrowers through the Public Service Loan Forgiveness (PSLF) Program, a debt forgiveness plan for public servants who completed 120 qualifying monthly payments.[6] But for progressive critics—namely, younger civil rights activists and left-of-center politicians—the administration's efforts, albeit noble, simply did not go far enough. They argued that the staggering student debt that borrowers faced called for a more radical and robust response. In the interest of fairness and equity, they contended that loan forgiveness should be extended across the board to all student borrowers, not just a select group of public service employees.

"All borrowers, including Direct Loan, Federal Family Education Loan (FFEL), graduate, and Parent PLUS borrowers, must be eligible for cancellation without regard to current borrower income, default status, or repayment plan," declared a coalition of civil rights organizations in a public statement that included representatives from the National Association for the Advancement of Colored People (NAACP), the Japanese American Citizens League, the National Urban League, UnidosUS, and the Leadership Conference on Civil and Human Rights. They added, "Whenever barriers are created for any relief program, all too often they exclude low-income and low-wealth individuals, even when the program was explicitly created to serve them."[7] The civil rights leaders charged that "data and research show that the burden of student debt for people of color includes all loan types, at all education levels, and at all income levels. Means-testing or limiting cancellation to only those borrowers who hold certain types of loans and degrees would deny relief to many struggling borrowers."[8]

There's little question that this series of loan forgiveness programs have undeniably helped millions of Americans clear their financial debt. However, many poor and working-class individuals, particularly from Black, Latinx, and other minoritized communities, still struggle today with overwhelming student debt. Given the ongoing discussions about the need to increase access to higher education, this book addresses a fundamental question that has persisted for the last three decades: Who gets to go to college? This inquiry is particularly relevant considering the raging national debate surrounding the rising costs of college education and the value of a college degree. The question deserves serious consideration as we examine the effectiveness of current policies and their impact on different demographic groups.

This book also examines the history and current state of the US student debt crisis, which continues to worsen without clear solutions. While 1960s political leaders like Congressman Adam Clayton Powell and Senator Claiborne Pell boldly championed accessible and affordable higher education initiatives for under-served populations, today's reality is stark, and the student debt issue has become a political football and hotly contested wedge issue. Of the forty-five million Americans who currently owe $1.7 trillion in student loan debt, women hold nearly two-thirds, struggling more with repayment due to gender pay disparities. The crisis disproportionately affects Black and Brown students, with Black women like Shauntee Russell graduating with an average of $38,000 in undergraduate debt. This severe impact on marginalized groups, particularly Black women, remains an underaddressed issue in the ongoing debate over effective policies to address the student debt crisis.[9]

Tiffany Jones of the Bill & Melinda Gates Foundation argues that the student debt crisis disproportionately affects Black students due to systemic inequalities. She contends, "It is not due to 'bad' decisions by borrowers, nor is it a random occurrence;

it is the result of racism and inequity manifesting themselves in systemic injustices such as income and wealth gaps, separate and unequal segregation, inequitable funding in education, and ineffective federal and state policy that student debt then compounds to make college unaffordable for Black students." Jones is right to call for an entirely new paradigm to "help build a future where Black students do not have to mortgage their futures to pay for college."[10]

Student debt has become one of the country's most pressing civil rights issues of our day. Indeed, if our nation is to remain competitive on the global stage, we must address this problem—we have a moral imperative to do so. This urgency must stretch from Congress to the White House, calling for coordinated action to resolve a burgeoning crisis that impacts millions of Americans and threatens our very economic future.

1 | THE HIDDEN CRISIS

Our higher education system is one of the things that makes America exceptional. There's no place else that has the assets we do when it comes to higher education. People from all over the world aspire to come here and study here. And that is a good thing.

President Barack Obama, speaking at the College Opportunity Summit in 2014

While much attention has been devoted to the burden of student loan debt that students will inherit after graduation, a critical aspect of the student financial crisis often goes overlooked: the struggles faced by students while still in school.

Over the past few decades, the cost of higher education has skyrocketed, outpacing inflation and wage growth. The numbers are both startling and alarming. According to the National Center for Education Statistics, between 1980 and 2020, the average tuition at public four-year institutions increased by 169 percent after adjusting for inflation. This dramatic rise has shifted much of the financial burden onto students and their families.[1] One key factor contributing to rising costs is the steady decline in state funding for public universities. As states have aggressively cut back on higher education budgets, institutions have been forced to raise tuition to make up for the difference. This trend has accelerated the financialization of higher education, with students bearing an ever-larger share of the cost.

While financial aid programs exist to help students manage these costs, they have not kept pace with rising expenses. The purchasing power of Pell Grants, for instance, has diminished significantly over time. In the 1975–76 academic year, the maximum Pell Grant covered 79 percent of the cost of attending a four-year public college. By 2017–18, it covered only 29 percent.[2]

BASIC NEED INSECURITIES

A shocking number of college students struggle with food insecurity, and those numbers have increasingly worsened across the years. A 2019 survey by the Hope Center for College, Community, and Justice found that 39 percent of students at four-year institutions experienced food insecurity in the prior thirty days.[3] Data released by the National Postsecondary Student Aid Study in August 2023 revealed that more than one in five undergraduate college students have experienced food insecurity, which is defined as the limited or uncertain availability of adequate food or the ability to obtain that food in a socially acceptable way. In total, that's about four million people "whose experience was invisible. It's staggering in a nation this wealthy,"[4] remarked Sara Goldrick-Rab, an expert on college affordability and college students' basic needs. She is also the author of *Paying the Price: College Costs, Financial Aid, and the Betrayal of the American Dream*. The National Postsecondary Student Aid study featured responses from nearly one hundred thousand students and found that 23 percent of undergraduates and 12 percent of graduate students have experienced food insecurity, rates that are far higher than those among the general American public. The study also revealed that 8 percent of undergraduates and 5 percent of graduate students have experienced homelessness. "There's an alarming percentage of students who are enduring physical and emotional trauma," warned Jeff Webster, director of research at Trellis Company, a nonprofit that conducts research about food insecurity in higher education. "But it also speaks to their resilience, that they believe so strongly in the mission of going to college and what that can do to transform their lives that they're willing to make the sacrifices."[5]

The cause of this rising crisis is what Goldrick-Rab, a prominent sociologist and columnist for *Diverse*, has rightly labeled "the new economics of college." She said that as the cost of living has surged, the increase has not been captured in colleges' calculations of student expenses. This has led to students getting less financial aid than they need. For example, 21 percent of students whose full financial need was considered met by grants were food insecure. "Their estimates are wrong," quipped Goldrick-Rab. "If I'm meeting someone who's going to go to college, I say add $10,000 a year to what you think it's going to cost."

Scholars like Goldrick-Rab have long lamented that government programs to feed people have historically excluded college students. "It's a lot harder to get SNAP if you're in college," she pointed out. "That's by design."[6] The findings from this government-sanctioned study—the first of its kind—are significant because they highlight the invisibility of a growing group of students who have been unable to access critical government services in a timely fashion. Food insecurity, for example, was highest at Historically Black Colleges and Universities (HBCUs; 39 percent) and at for-profit colleges and universities (32 percent). But it was present at all kinds of institutions, including public four-years (22 percent) and private four-years (18 percent), countering the perception that food insecurity is mostly an issue for schools that serve predominantly lower-income students. There were also significant disparities by race. Food insecurity affected 35 percent of Black students, 30 percent of Native American students, and 25 percent of Latinx students, as well as 18 percent of whites and Asians. There were similar patterns in homelessness. Goldrick-Rab and other experts have attributed these differences to several factors, predominantly the widening wealth gap between Black, Indigenous, People of Color (BIPOC) and white families. "In terms of stereotypes that people have of how students end up in these situations, they tend to think that it's students who don't do the FAFSA [Free Application for Federal Student Aid], who don't apply for things, who have a too-high price for college that's partly their fault,"[7] said Goldrick-Rab. However, the data indicated that although 31 percent of Pell recipients had food insecurity, 17 percent of non-Pell recipients did as well. The data have also revealed that many students who had jobs were still hungry and 25 percent of students who worked twenty to thirty-nine hours a week reported food insecurity, as did 21 percent of those who worked forty hours a week or more. "The kinds of jobs [these students] can get just don't pay enough," said Goldrick-Rab. "A lot of those people have a lot of debt already. So, they're working, but they have a lot of bills." The expenses can be such that even those students from families that earned over $132,000 per year were affected. In fact, 11 percent of them reported food insecurity.

And good grades—while laudable—was not a factor in determining which students were hungry and which ones were not. About 18 percent of the students surveyed who had high school grade point averages (GPAs) above a 3.0 reported that they did not have enough food access. "This kind of poverty is not about lacking talent," said Goldrick-Rab. "Being a smart person and doing well in high school does not shield you completely from falling on hard times in college."[8]

The 2019 survey conducted by the Hope Center for College, Community, and Justice, which was founded by Goldrick-Rab, also revealed that 46 percent of students experienced some form of housing insecurity, with 17 percent facing homelessness in the previous year. These students were forced to couch surf, live in their cars, or stay in shelters, all while pursuing a college degree and/or credential.

TEXTBOOK COSTS

Equally concerning is the rising cost of textbooks and other course materials that college students were expected to purchase for their classes. The College Board estimated that students budgeted an average of $1,240 for books and supplies in the 2021–22 academic year. However, many students also reported skipping required textbook purchases or taking fewer courses to manage these high costs.[9] To make ends meet, many of these same students had to hold down employment while attending college—sometimes working more than one job.

According to the National Center for Education Statistics, more than 40 percent of full-time undergraduate students in the United States and 81 percent of part-time students are employed while enrolled as students, significantly impacting their academic performance. The grades for students who worked more than fifteen to twenty hours tended to suffer, and this group of students was more at risk of dropping out of college.

Jamie Wood's college experience reveals a lesser-known barrier to higher education: the staggering cost of textbooks. Wood, a bright-eyed first-year student at a Portland, Oregon, university, arrived on campus in the fall of 2023 full of hope and ambition. However, he quickly encountered a financial hurdle he hadn't anticipated. "When I saw the price tag for my textbooks, my heart sank," Wood recalled, his voice tinged with frustration. "It was over $1,500 for just one semester. That's more than I make in a month at my part-time job."[10]

Faced with this unexpected expense, Wood made a difficult decision. He chose not to purchase any of his required textbooks, hoping to find alternative ways to access the material. "I thought I could manage," he explained. "I figured I'd borrow books from classmates or find the information online. I was wrong."

Wood's story is far from unique. According to a recent survey by the US Public Interest Research Group, 65 percent of students have skipped buying a textbook due to cost, even if they were concerned it would hurt their grade.[11] As the semester progressed, Wood found himself falling behind in his classes. He tried to borrow textbooks from classmates, when possible, but coordinating schedules and sharing limited resources proved challenging. "It was embarrassing," he said. "I felt like I was always asking for help, always behind. I didn't want my classmates or professors to know I couldn't afford the books."

Wood's reluctance to discuss his situation with his professors is common among students facing financial difficulties. Many, like Wood, feel a sense of shame or fear of judgment. "I thought about asking my professors to put the books on reserve in the library," he said, "but I was too embarrassed. I didn't want them to think I wasn't serious about my studies." As the weeks went by, Wood fell further behind. Eventually, he found himself unable to complete readings at all, severely impacting his academic performance. "It was a snowball effect," he explained. "Missing one reading led to missing another, and soon I was completely lost in some of my classes."

The irony of the situation wasn't lost on Wood. In some classes, professors assigned only a few chapters from textbooks costing eighty-five dollars or more. "It felt like such a waste," he said, shaking his head in frustration. "Paying that much for a book we barely used. It just didn't make sense." It was during a late-night study session, desperately trying to catch up on missed material, that Wood first heard about open educational resources (OER) from a classmate. "When they explained what OER was, it sounded too good to be true," he recalled. "Free, openly licensed educational materials that everyone can access? That could have changed everything for me if I knew about it earlier."

Open educational resources are teaching, learning, and research materials that are either in the public domain or released with intellectual property licenses that allow for free use, adaptation, and distribution. They can include textbooks, curricula, lecture notes, assignments, tests, projects, audio, video, and animation. For students like Wood, OER represents a potential solution to the textbook affordability crisis. By providing free access to high-quality educational materials, OER could level the playing field for students from all economic backgrounds. "If all of my professors had used OER, I wouldn't have fallen behind," Wood said. "I could have accessed all the materials from day one, just like everyone else."

Wood's experience has turned him into an advocate for OER and textbook affordability. He's become active in the student government association and has started to speak out about his own experience, hoping to raise awareness about the issue among both students and faculty. "People don't realize how much textbook costs can impact a student's success," Wood said. "It's not just about the money. It's about access to education, about having an equal opportunity to learn and succeed."

As conversations about college affordability continue to focus on tuition and student loans, stories like Wood's highlight the need to address other costs associated with higher education. The textbook industry, which has seen prices rise at three times the rate of inflation over the last four decades, is increasingly coming under scrutiny. Some institutions and states are taking notice. Several colleges have launched OER initiatives, and some states have passed legislation to promote the use of open educational resources. However, widespread adoption remains a challenge. "I don't want other students to go through what I did," Wood said. "Education should be about learning, not about whether you can afford a textbook."

HIDDEN COSTS AND MENTAL HEALTH

Experts whose research focuses on college students have long warned of the stress that students like Wood experience, particularly when it comes to juggling work, academic studies, and financial worries. All those factors tend to take a dramatic toll on a student's mental health. We've seen that anxiety and depression rates among college students who have experienced financial stress are also on the rise.

Maria Sanchez, thirty-one, knows this reality all too well. She is a full-time third-year nursing student who works approximately 37.5 hours a week as a nanny to support herself while also contributing to her family's expenses. A first-generation Latina, Sanchez often skips meals to save money and accesses the classroom textbooks on loan at the library because she cannot afford to purchase new or used copies. While she has remained committed to her studies and has worked to keep a 3.1 GPA, her grades have admittedly slipped as she has struggled to balance both her school and work duties. "It is not easy," she confessed. "I would love the opportunity to just focus on being a student instead of taking care of a small child who is not even mine all day, but that is not possible. I must work and it feels very stressful because I am unable to give my all to my schoolwork in the way that I would like to. I feel like I am constantly falling behind."[12] Her student loan debt is also piling up, as she's had to borrow $15,000 each year to pay for her education. "It feels like I'm working just to pay off bills," she told me. "I work so much that I can't even enjoy life. It's the same routine every day."

Like Sanchez, Robert Carroll is a dedicated student. But he is not the first in his family to attend college. Three generations of his family members have gone on to college and have earned college degrees. From the time he was young, the same was expected of him. "Going to college was never even up for discussion," said Carroll, nineteen, a second-year biology student at a private four-year college. He hails from a middle-class white family and was raised in central Ohio. "Going to college was just something that my parents, guidance counselors, teachers, and people in my community and at church drilled into me from the very beginning of my existence." Carroll's first year in college went smoothly. He received enough financial aid to help offset the cost of his tuition and fees and got involved in the school's student government association and the drama club. He ended his first year with a solid 3.8 GPA. But then, his father lost his job, and the family was unable to pay the outstanding balance to cover his dorm and meal plan. Being four hours from his home, he was unable to move back in with his parents and commute to and from school. "So, I had to give up my dorm and my meal plan and now I just stay with a whole bunch of different friends, alternating between their couches,"[13] he said. "When the couch is unavailable, I just crash on somebody's floor." Increasingly, more college students are finding themselves in situations that are like Carroll's. These students couch surf, and in some instances, they also sleep in their cars or seek housing in shelters while also trying to earn a college degree.

Joselin Williamson, twenty, a young African American woman, has been holding down three part-time jobs while trying to earn her associate's degree at a community college located in the northeast. Williamson works at a department store in the mornings and a fast-food restaurant in the afternoons and drives Uber and Lyft—the popular ride-sharing car services—in the evenings and during the weekends. She squeezes in her studies whenever she has a free moment but finds that she often must ask her instructors for extensions on assignments. "I would prefer not to have to work so much just to earn a dollar," she said. "I wish I had the luxury of just being a student, but I have bills to pay. I don't want to drop out because I really don't trust myself to ever return to school if I do that. If I drop out, I know that I will prob-ably never finish my degree and I promised my grandma before she died that I would one day become a college graduate. She never had that opportunity."[14]

As of 2022, the Some College, No Credential (SCNC) popu-lation in the United States under the age of sixty-five has soared to about 36.8 million.[15] These are individuals who have received some postsecondary education but stopped out for a variety of reasons. Even though they may have paid some of the costs asso-ciated with being a college student, they do not have an earned credential or certificate, yet they are still on the hook for paying back the loans. It's the financial pressures like those experienced by Sanchez, Carroll, and Williamson that have forced so many students to dramatically reduce their course load, take semesters off, or drop out of college completely. We know that over the long run, a decision by a student to delay their graduation not only prolongs their time in school but also increases the total cost of their education. Additionally, students who must prioritize imme-diate earnings over internships or other career-building opportu-nities too often find themselves at a disadvantage when entering the job market after graduation. These financial challenges only exacerbate existing socioeconomic inequalities, making it much harder for students from low-income backgrounds to achieve upward mobility through higher education.

In response to this growing trend, colleges and universities have established food pantries and emergency aid programs to help students in acute financial distress. While helpful, these programs often struggle to meet the full extent of student needs, and the services provided tend to vary greatly from institution to institution. Federal and institutional work-study programs have also helped students to secure flexible, on-campus employment. However, the funding for these programs has been limited and has not kept pace with the demand. Over the past decade, more institutions have readily embraced the use of open educational resources to reduce textbook costs. These freely accessible, openly licensed materials have significantly decreased the financial burden on students. But once again, institutions have varying policies on the implementation of OER on their campuses and some instructors have remained resistant to utilizing these resources.

UNPAID STUDENT BALANCES

Nationally, about 6.6 million students have been identified as having stranded credits. These are credits students have earned but cannot access because of their unpaid balance with a college that they once attended, which is holding their transcript as collateral. City College of New York (CUNY) and the State University of New York (SUNY)—two of the largest college systems in the nation—changed its policy and no longer holds a transcript of a student who has earned the degree but has an outstanding bill.[16] In the wake of the COVID-19 pandemic, many institutions (including my own—Trinity Washington University) settled more than $1.8 million in student balances for nearly four hundred full-time undergraduate students in the summer of 2021. Using federal funds from the American Rescue Plan, the Predominantly Black Institution (PBI) and the Hispanic-Serving Institution (HSI) located in the nation's capital paid off 40 percent of the full-time undergraduate student body debt, with the average balance payoff being about $4,583. "This is absolutely the right thing to do for our students," said Trinity's president, Patricia McGuire. "Trinity students will start the Fall 2021 semester with a fresh balance sheet on their Trinity accounts," she said. "Many of our students lost their jobs at restaurants and other service locations, and others were also the primary financial support for their families, making it hard to pay their tuition bills."

While students could have registered for the next semester, they still had balances. So, McGuire used the funds provided through the American Rescue Plan that allowed colleges and universities to resolve student balances that were accrued during the global pandemic. "We want to wipe the slate clean so they can start the fall semester with a zero Trinity balance," McGuire, who has led the private, historically women's Catholic university since 1989, said at the time. The gesture aligned to the school-wide initiative called Trinity DARE: Driving Actions for Racial Equity, which was created to focus on specific strategies and actions to promote racial equity for Trinity students and graduates.

"We believe that widening pipelines for our graduates to enter professions where persons of color are under-represented is one of the strongest contributions Trinity can make to improving the climate for racial equity more broadly," said McGuire. "Black women carry the highest student debt burden in the country, and debt loads often inhibit their ability to complete degrees and become successful in their chosen professions. Reducing student debt burdens hastens degree completion and supports early career success, which ensures long-term growth and professional achievement."[17]

MORE DISPARITIES

While stopgap measures provide some temporary relief to the financial hardships faced by students, broader systemic change is clearly needed. There's no question that higher education institutions need more state and federal funding to help offset tuition increases. Expanding need-based grant programs to cover a larger portion of college costs must become the norm. In addition, institutions must address the rising costs of living, especially in college towns. Colleges and universities, working in tandem with the federal government, must provide comprehensive financial literacy programs for students and their families to ensure that everyone understands the investment and costs associated with earning a college education.

COVID-19 highlighted and exacerbated the digital divide that exists among today's college students. At the height of the pandemic, when colleges and universities shut their doors, sent college students home, and pivoted to online learning, we discovered that many students lacked reliable access to computers or high-speed internet, creating significant barriers to their education. The Alabama State University president, Quinton Ross, lamented that he had students who lived in rural areas where broadband internet just wasn't available. They had to "complete their coursework using the old correspondence course."[18] The transition to online learning wasn't seamless for everyone. It introduced new costs for students, including the need for upgraded technology, better internet connections, and quiet spaces to attend virtual classes. The pandemic highlighted the widening economic disparities that exist between the haves and the have nots.

In recent years, more attention has been focused on the challenges that student parents face as they pursue their education and balance the expenses of raising children. The high cost of childcare has proved prohibitive for student parents, often exceeding the cost of tuition. Nicole Lynn Lewis, founder and chief executive officer of Generation Hope, a nonprofit organization that supports student parents and their children, has helped to bring public awareness to this issue. The author of *Pregnant Girl: A Story of Teen Motherhood, College, and Creating a Better Future for Young Families*, Lewis described her experiences as a teen mother and student at William & Mary.[19] She has noted that student parents must balance coursework, employment, and family responsibilities, often leading to extreme stress and time poverty. They often miss out on networking opportunities, internships, and other career-building experiences due to these responsibilities.

Like student parents, another invisible student population is international students, who often face enormous challenges. While there has long been a myth that students who come to the United States to study often have the financial means to be able to do so, we know that a sizable number of international students struggle financially. They face visa restrictions and higher tuition rates and are ineligible for federal financial aid. Visa regulations typically limit their ability to work off campus, restricting their options for earning income.

As more students struggle to meet their basic needs while pursuing their degrees, the promise of higher education as a path to upward mobility will remain under constant threat. Addressing these challenges will require concerted effort from policymakers, institutions, and society at large. Only by ensuring that students can focus on their studies without the constant stress of financial insecurity can we hope to realize the full potential of a college education.

2 | A CIVIL RIGHTS ISSUE
A Moral Imperative

> A day after the Supreme Court stuck a knife in the back of Black America, a majority of justices have now cut the ladder out from under us. Generations of Black youth were sold a bill of goods that higher education was a pathway out of poverty—only to be saddled with crushing debt that never lets them see their dreams fully realized.
>
> Reverend Al Sharpton, National Action Network founder and president, speaking to reporters in 2022

Just as 250,000 Americans had journeyed to the nation's capital sixty years earlier for the historic 1963 March on Washington for Jobs and Freedom, a new generation of marchers returned to Washington, DC, in 2023 to continue the call for change. This time, student debt was among the many civil rights issues weighing on people's minds.

The protesters gathered on the National Mall with an urgent demand: they wanted Congress and President Biden to address the out-of-control student debt crisis, even as they worked to safeguard voting rights and eliminate police brutality by calling for the passage of the George Floyd Justice in Policing Act. Despite the oppressive heat, which climbed into the nineties on that unusually warm August day, scores of college students turned out in record numbers for the "Not a Commemoration, A Continuation" march. Organized by civil rights leader and MSNBC host Reverend Al Sharpton, participants came from historically Black colleges and universities (HBCUs), community colleges, for-profit institutions, and elite universities like Harvard, Cornell, and Yale to take a stand.

The stakes were high this time around. Just two months earlier, the US Supreme Court had brazenly struck down affirmative action and President Biden's plan to cancel student loans in a one-two punch. "They will live under these decisions longer than many of us convening the march," Sharpton told me on the eve of the event, as he prepared to deliver a powerful message before tens of thousands of marchers who would assemble at the Lincoln Memorial before marching to the King Memorial just a short distance away. Sharpton predicted that the erosion of voting rights and the Republican attacks on affirmative action and the student loan forgiveness program would inevitably drive droves of young people to the polls in the 2024 presidential election— regardless of who was on the top of the ticket. "Where has the reaction been to these assaults?" he asked, pacing back and forth in his hotel room. "There has been no collective action."[1]

In the wake of these Supreme Court rulings, Sharpton warned that America's college students "will have fewer rights than what I grew up with."[2] Sharpton, who has emerged as the nation's most prominent civil rights leader, began his activism at the age of thirteen when he was appointed to serve as the youth leader of the New York chapter of Operation Breadbasket, the economic arm of Dr. Martin Luther King Jr.'s Southern Christian Leadership Conference (SCLC). After graduating from Samuel J. Tilden High School, the New York native enrolled at Brooklyn College but eventually dropped out—much to the chagrin of his mentors—to focus exclusively on his civil rights work full-time. Sharpton continued, however, to support access to college education through the National Youth Movement, the civil rights group he founded in 1971 with a $500 donation from civil rights and labor leader Bayard Rustin, one of the architects of the 1963 March on Washington.

In the late 1960s and early 1970s, the fight for racial equality was being pursued on multiple fronts. A key strategy focused on securing civil and human rights for Black Americans through economic empowerment, despite differing ideologies and approaches. The Black Panther Party, which was more militant than the integrationist and nonviolent philosophy of the SCLC and its youth arm, the Student Nonviolent Coordinating Committee (SNCC), advocated for a Ten-Point Program that included economic equality. The Nation of Islam, under Elijah Muhammad, called for the creation of a Black capitalist structure independent of white dependency. In contrast, the SCLC's Operation Breadbasket, led nationally by Reverend Jesse Louis Jackson Sr., a charismatic lieutenant to Dr. King, promoted various economic incentives for the Black community, including the employment of African Americans by companies operating in Black neighborhoods. Adopting a tactical strategy known as "selective patronage," Breadbasket activists organized continuous boycotts and demonstrations against companies that overlooked their Black consumers. These early experiences of focusing on economic and racial justice left a lasting impression on Sharpton, who understood that the fight for civil rights had to be multiracial and closely linked to the fight for economic mobility.

The ongoing student debt crisis, which disenfranchises millions of Americans from achieving economic freedom, had now become a key issue in the ever-evolving and ever-expanding civil rights movement. "Generations of Black youth were sold the idea that higher education was a pathway out of poverty, only to be burdened with crushing debt that prevents them from fully realizing their dreams,"[3] said Sharpton. He noted that it was not a coincidence that the Supreme Court's 2023 ruling striking down Biden's student debt relief plan came shortly after the court's decision to dismantle affirmative action, effectively banning the consideration of race in college admissions. "They have targeted college students, either by blocking their access to elite institutions or by placing a financial burden on them so heavy that they can't succeed,"[4] he added.

STUDENT FREEDOM INITIATIVE

In the crowd at the 2023 march in DC was billionaire Robert F. Smith. A 1985 graduate of Cornell University with a degree in chemical engineering, Smith later earned an MBA from Columbia Business School and began his career as an investment banker at Goldman Sachs. However, it was his role as the founder, chair, and CEO of Vista Equity Partners—a global investment firm—that would bring him widespread recognition and catapult him onto a more prominent stage. Smith used this prominence and his fortune to draw attention to the burgeoning student debt crisis. In a noble act of philanthropy, he announced during a 2019 commencement speech at Dr. Martin Luther King

Jr.'s alma mater—Morehouse College—that he and his family would donate $34 million to pay off the student debt of every Morehouse graduate from that year.

"Men of Morehouse, you are surrounded by a community of people who have helped you arrive at this sacred place on this sacred day," Smith told the graduates from the platform stage, wearing a doctoral robe bearing the school's historic colors— maroon and white. "On behalf of the eight generations of my family who have been in this country, we are going to put a little fuel in your bus."[5] The "fuel" that Smith referenced during his speech made headlines and was celebrated worldwide. For the Morehouse graduates, however, Smith's philanthropic investment meant much more than just a flashy news story. It signified the sudden removal of a heavy financial burden as they readied themselves to enter the workforce or to continue their studies. "Just imagine the weight lifted off your shoulders when you have a clean slate coming out of college," said Dwytt Lewis, who graduated from Morehouse with a degree in business administration. Thanks to Smith's generosity, his $150,000 debt was wiped away in a blink of an eye.[6]

Smith's investment in these Morehouse men came at a time when economists warned that national student loan debt had skyrocketed to around $1.7 trillion, with the average student accumulating approximately $33,000 in loans. Following his 2019 gift to Morehouse College, Smith wanted to do more than to just make a one-time donation. He expanded his philanthropic efforts into a broader movement by founding the Student Freedom Initiative (SFI). This national nonprofit would provide a scalable solution to the growing student loan debt crisis, with a particular focus on HBCUs. SFI would offer juniors and seniors studying science, technology, engineering, and mathematics (STEM) at an HBCU with a flexible alternative to high-interest private student loans. These low-interest loans would be repaid after graduation on a scale based on the student's income. "Dr. King knew that economic rights were the key to true equality," Smith told marchers during his six-minute primetime speech in 2023 that was televised around the world. "He once asked, 'What does it profit a man to eat at an integrated lunch counter if he does not earn enough money to buy a hamburger and a cup of coffee?'"

During his speech, Smith recalled that during the summer of 1963, when he was just nine months old, his mother, Sylvia, took him and his brother on the seventeen-hundred-mile journey from Denver to Washington, DC, to experience history in the making. They were joined by thousands of others to witness Dr. King deliver his iconic "I Have a Dream" speech. "My mother knew that her boys would be too young to remember that speech, but she believed that the history we witnessed that day on the National Mall would always be a part of the men we would one day become," Smith said. "And Mom was right, as usual. I still feel that day in my bones, and it echoes all around us here at Morehouse."

The symbolism of that moment between Smith and the Morehouse graduates was palpable and profound. The students clinched onto every word that Smith uttered. Here was the richest Black man in America, standing on the campus that counts Dr. King as its most famous alumnus, offering these newly minted graduates with the biggest gift they could ever imagine: the opportunity to start their postcollege lives completely debt-free. Determined to invest in the limitless potential of the next generation, Smith was looking to end the cycle in which Black

Americans remained "symbolic sharecroppers" and "impoverished tenants in someone else's land."[7]

This was what the civil rights movement was all about.

"END STUDENT LOAN DEBT NOW"

Two months before the activists gathered in DC for the "Not a Commemoration, A Continuation" march, Tylik McMillan was anxiously awaiting the US Supreme Court's ruling on President Joe Biden's student loan debt relief program. There was much on the line, especially after the court overturned *Roe v. Wade* and dismantled affirmative action. As a youth activist for Sharpton's National Action Network, McMillan had campaigned tirelessly to raise awareness about the student debt crisis, which he viewed as a critical civil rights issue. "Student debt has been at the top of Gen Z's agenda as we talk about equitable education, as we talk about fair education and access," he explained.[8]

Reflecting on his challenging upbringing in Harrisburg, Pennsylvania, and Lawrenceville, Virginia, McMillan recalled the uncertainty he faced regarding his own educational future. With a mother battling cancer and an incarcerated father, college seemed out of reach for McMillan as he was preparing to graduate from high school. "I'm thinking, 'We already don't have a lot as it is, so how can I afford to go to a four-year university?'" he remembered.[9] Initially considering the military as his only option, McMillan's path changed thanks in part to his mother's encouragement that he go on to college. "Luckily, I had a mother who believed in me and wanted me to achieve my dreams," he said.[10] "She knew that college would be the best bet for me and encouraged me to attend."

McMillan enrolled at North Carolina Agricultural and Technical State University (NC A&T) in Greensboro, the nation's largest HBCU with over thirteen thousand students. The school's rich civil rights history captivated McMillan, particularly its connection to figures like the Reverend Jesse Louis Jackson Sr. and the "Greensboro Four"—Ezell Blair Jr., Franklin McCain, Joseph McNeil, and David Richmond. These four A&T students ignited a national movement on February 1, 1960, when they courageously sat down at the whites-only lunch counter of F. W. Woolworth's and refused to leave until closing time despite being denied service. Their actions inspired similar sit-ins across the country, elevating the civil rights movement beyond its traditional leadership of Black Baptist preachers. This wave of student activism led to the formation of SNCC during a planning meeting at Shaw University, another HBCU in nearby Raleigh, North Carolina. In the years since its formation, SNCC quickly nurtured future leaders like John Lewis, who would go on to become a congressman from Georgia; Marion Barry, who would become the long-serving mayor of Washington, DC, and activist Stokely Carmichael (later Kwame Ture), all pivotal figures in the civil rights and Black Power movements.

Much to McMillan's surprise, shortly after he applied, NC A&T not only offered him a seat in their first-year class but also gave him an impressive Reserve Officer's Training Corps (ROTC) scholarship that covered the full cost of his tuition. He was elated. Finally, he thought, this was his opportunity to pursue a college education at virtually no cost. But by the time his sophomore year rolled around, McMillan had grown alarmed by what he saw happening in the overall society. A spate of police killings of unarmed Black men motivated him to take up the mantle of civil rights, just like those who came before him in the 1960s. But not everyone was excited about his activism. "My commander at the time told me that I couldn't mix politics and the military, so I had to make a decision about what I wanted to do," remembered McMillan, who decided to turn down the ROTC scholarship. "I decided to follow my heart, and I ended up losing the scholarship and having to pay it all back. This put my family in a financial bind."

Because McMillan had emerged as a visible student leader on campus, the school's administrators tried their best to help him secure other need-based grants so that he wouldn't have to drop out of school and return to Virginia. But in the end, the assistance wasn't enough. McMillan found himself shelling out about $1,000 a month to defray the cost of tuition and boarding. Finances, he recalled, were unusually tight because of his family's socioeconomic background. "There were many times that I thought I would have to drop out of college because there was no money for books, tuition, housing, travel," he said. It's these additional expenses that students face—even beyond the rising tuition costs—that McMillan has argued should be the motivation for a renewed national conversation focused on student debt cancellation.

Just a week before the Supreme Court announced their ruling on Biden's student debt relief program, dozens of activists representing civil rights organizations from across the nation gathered outside of the White House to generate media attention on the debt crisis, which they felt had been woefully undercovered in the major networks. They had descended from across the country onto the nation's capital, one by one, to urge the Biden administration to take whatever measures were needed to ensure that the millions of borrowers who were counting on some form of student debt relief that had been promised to them during the 2020 presidential campaign ultimately received it.

"End Student Loan Debt Now," they chanted loudly as they marched their way up DC's Pennsylvania Avenue, hoping that Biden would hear their plea through the windows of the Oval Office. But why, some wondered, were these young activists even at the White House to begin with, when the fate of the student debt relief program was now squarely in the hands of the Supreme Court some two miles away? "Our message to President Biden is clear: failure is not an option, and swift, decisive action is demanded," declared Wisdom O. Cole, the national director of the NAACP Youth & College Division. "Young Black borrowers are expecting this president to show up for them in the same way they have mobilized for him."[11] The demand from these young activists was resoundingly clear: Biden needed to do something quickly in the likely event that the court's conservative majority rejected his plan. But as the chants died down and the marching came to a halt, it wasn't precisely clear what more the president could do. Still, the activists had their suspicions almost from the start of the Biden administration that the president had not prioritized this issue. There had long been lingering questions even when Biden was a presidential candidate over how committed he was to the student debt relief movement. They noticed that during the Democratic primary back in 2020, he showed up noticeably late to the national conversation and was initially skeptical and reluctant to propose any debt forgiveness plan. It was only after the progressive wing of the Democratic Party pushed him to take up the cause that he developed a plan that eventually morphed into his New Deal of sorts. What he ultimately settled on excited anxious borrowers, particularly first-generation, minoritized, and recent college graduates who, despite having earned their college degree, struggled to keep pace with the payments and accruing interests on their loans. They were feeling the financial pain in their wallets and pocketbooks, and Biden—ever the dutiful politician—provided the rhetorical comfort that they needed to hear to convince them that everything would be alright. "You get all these degrees, and you get all this debt, and you get in a position where you can't get a job because no one is hiring, or they're hiring at very low wages . . . I'm going to eliminate your student debt if you come from a family [making less] than $125,000 and went to a public university," he sounded off to thunderous applause, as he crisscrossed the nation back in 2020 in search of votes.[12]

Cole and the other activists had remembered those fiery speeches from the campaign trail. Like their civil rights forefathers and foremothers some sixty years earlier, they decided to use both their chants and their feet to send a signal to the now elected and governing president that they were going to hold him and his administration squarely accountable, regardless of what the high court decided to do. "We are here today with a plan, telling President Biden it is time to follow through. It is not done until it's done," Cole said at that June protest that drew hundreds into the streets on a humid DC evening. "It's not just enough that we pause time after time and time again, we have to see that relief. We have to see that plan come through."[13] The response of these activists was much more confrontational than that of some of the established Black elders, civil rights leaders, and power brokers, who took a more measured tone in addressing the student loan issue with Biden. But respectability politics aside,

Cole viewed the student debt as part of a broader civil rights and equity issue that was at the heart of the lingering racial wealth gap that crippled the nation. It was an issue that young people were galvanized around just a year ahead of the 2024 presidential election. Biden, Cole warned, had to act. "If the president and administration truly care about equity, truly care about Black people, truly care about the future of this nation and the opportunity for economic mobility, then they will come through on this plan and reassure the American public that something will get done."[14]

By the time that McMillan finally got word, just a week later, that the Supreme Court had killed Biden's plan to provide the forty million student loan borrowers who had hoped to have a portion of their federal student debt permanently forgiven, he was already in organizing mode, focused on the future. The twenty-six-year-old activist had learned from his mentor, the Reverend Al Sharpton, that you lose some fights, you win some, but civil rights activism required an endurance that needed to be sustained over the long haul. McMillan was now focused on the marathon and had shifted his attention to mobilizing voters for the 2024 presidential election. "This is a temporary stumbling block," he told me, no longer anxious but eager to put the issue before voters in the 2024 election. "This is not going to fade away. We are not going to go away. If anything, young voters are going to turn out in record numbers in 2024 because they're passionate about police reform, voting rights, and student debt. There will be even more determination despite this defeat. We're now pushing for reparations."

3 | REPARATIONS AND STUDENT DEBT

The easy fix is to cancel student debt. That's a reparation because education was not afforded to Black people in this country. So, when education for Black Americans was afforded, there came a price tag, a higher price tag than most have to pay.

Keisha Deonarine, NAACP director of opportunity, race and justice, speaking to reporters in January 2024

In 2019, Texas Congresswoman Sheila Jackson Lee reintroduced H.R. 40, a controversial piece of legislation in Congress that quickly got Americans talking openly about race, restorative social justice, and repair. The nation was still in the throes of a Donald J. Trump presidency, which two years earlier witnessed white supremacists storm through the streets of Charlottesville, Virginia, angrily chanting "White Lives Matter" and "Jews will not replace us!" Carrying tiki torches, swastikas, and semi-automatics, they marched toward a statue of General Robert E. Lee, who defiantly fought on the side of the Confederacy during the Civil War to defend and maintain American slavery at all costs. The day-long march culminated in the death of thirty-two-year-old Heather Heyer, a counterprotester who was struck and killed by a rabid racist who drove his car into a busy crowd. When President Trump was later asked about the angry mob and their incendiary rhetoric during a televised national press conference, he remarked that there were "very fine people on both sides"[1] of the protests. That horrific episode, along with a decision by some colleges, universities, and city governments to tear down the statues of Confederate leaders and former slave owners who espoused racist views, only broadened the national conversation about the role of reparations as a remedy to help bring about a national racial reckoning.

And then a year later, the murder of George Floyd at the hands of a white Minneapolis police officer further prompted calls for racial justice and triggered around-the-clock protests that erupted in cities across the world. Bandied about during all these direct-action protests was a demand that student debt forgiveness for Black Americans should also be included in any push for reparations. And for a short time, we saw institutions respond to the protests. Scholarships were created to help even the playing field for African American students. Colleges and universities embraced the hiring of chief diversity officers and promised to hire more faculty of color. But those efforts proved to be short-lived. By 2024, an anti-diversity movement was in full swing that caused many institutions—particularly public colleges and universities—to renege on their previous commitments.

For many, H.R. 40 was the modern-day answer to a historical wound that had never fully healed. Jackson Lee's legislation called for a thirteen-person federal commission to study American slavery and its lingering effects and to offer suggestions on what government could do to mitigate those effects. After the completion of its study, the commission would then be required to issue recommendations about possible "forms of rehabilitation or restitution"—essentially, reparations—to Congress. "While it might be convenient to assume that we can address the current divisive racial and political climate in our nation through race-neutral means, experience shows that we have not escaped our history," Jackson Lee said at the time. "Though the civil rights movement challenged many of the most racist practices and structures that subjugated the African American community, it was not followed by a commitment to truth and reconciliation. For that reason, the legacy of racial inequality has persisted and left the nation vulnerable to a range of problems that continue to yield division, racial disparities, and injustice."

H.R. 40, Jackson Lee promised, could "start a movement toward the national reckoning we need to bridge racial divides." Reparations, she added, "are ultimately about respect and reconciliation—and the hope that one day, all Americans can walk together toward a more just future."[2] Along with a pledge to tackle the student debt crisis, Biden had also promised on the 2020 presidential campaign trail to create a commission to study reparations. The prospects for the legislation initially appeared hopeful. In 2021, the House Judiciary Committee voted to bring H.R. 40 out of committee—a historic feat for the legislation that had been viewed as fringe from the moment that Rep. John Conyers of Michigan introduced the first version of the bill in 1989. Back then, Conyers forcefully argued that the United States needed to account for the brutal mistreatment of African Americans during the period of chattel slavery, and Jim Crow segregation, which resulted in the ongoing forms of racism that continued to permeate our society.

A MORAL AND THEOLOGICAL IMPERATIVE

While Jackson Lee's resurrected legislation was heralded by some, including mainstream civil rights groups like the NAACP, National Action Network, and the National Urban League, it was predictably denounced by others. According to a 2021 Pew Research Center survey, only three in ten US adults believe that the descendants of slavery in the US should be repaid in some way, such as through land or money. About seven in ten (68 percent) disagreed.[3] There has been a seismic shift among predominantly white institutions over the past two decades—prompted in part by progressive white students—who started to question their institution's role in slavery and the exclusion of Black students across the decade After pressure from its study body, Georgetown University announced in 2019 that it would fundraise $400,000 a year to create a fund that would benefit the descendants of 247 slaves sold by the school's Jesuit founders in 1833. The money has since been used to fund community projects like schools and health clinics for the over four thousand living Black descendants. The Jesuit Conference of Canada and the United States, which played an instrumental role in the founding of Georgetown—the nation's oldest Catholic school—also pledged $100 million toward a $1 billion goal to support the education of descendants.

Georgetown's announcement came on the heels of similar gestures that were made by Princeton Theological Seminary and Virginia Theological Seminary. Princeton Theological Seminary offered $27 million toward scholarships and related projects to descendants, while Virginia Theological Seminary created a $1.7 million reparations fund. In 2021, a decade after

Brown University released a report that confirmed its ties to slavery, its undergraduate students cast a historic vote in favor of reparations.

These actions on college campuses provided Jackson Lee with the green light that she needed to drive the reparations debate forward. It also sparked a critical debate in society at large about what restitution meant and how much, if anything, was enough. For religiously affiliated higher education institutions in particular, reparations also involved another layer of dialogue: struggling with not only their tangled financial past but also their theological contributions to slavery. Didn't they have a moral obligation to tackle the issue head-on? "People have to wrestle with the fact that many of these institutions produced pro-slavery theologians," Dr. Yolanda Pierce, the former dean of Howard University's divinity school who is now at Vanderbilt University, told *Diverse: Issues In Higher Education* back in 2019. "It isn't that we're just simply talking about people who physically held people in bondage, though there were plenty of them," she added, noting that theologians, pastors, and priests at many of these institutions would go on to write proslavery theology. "I think there is and there has to be a wrestling with that history."[4]

It's a complicated history for sure. While some Christian denominations broke away to reject slavery, some saw the mere existence of slavery in the Old Testament as justification for it, while others pointed to New Testament texts that idealized servitude, like "Servants be obedient to them that are your masters," from Paul's letter to the Ephesians. According to Dr. Terrence Johnson, professor of African American Religious Studies at Harvard Divinity School, these texts were taught to slaves by Christian owners to "point to this idea that if you were obedient, heaven is your reward." Slaves simultaneously looked to texts like the exodus story for hope, so much so that scholars have found Bibles that were provided to slaves with the exodus story cut out. Johnson said some Jesuits—the Catholic order that founded my alma mater, Georgetown University, in 1789—held that African Americans had souls and could be saved, an "enlightened" view at the time. But they still owned slaves themselves, while several Protestant sects fused racial pseudoscience with religious texts to paint slaves as "innately inferior."[5] When America's oldest universities were founded, theological justifications for slavery were a regular part of conversations happening in biblical studies classrooms. The reverberations of those debates are still felt on campuses.

Nicholas Young, who was president of the Association of Black Seminarians at Princeton Theological Seminary in 2019, used his tenure at the helm to advocate for broader reflection that not only focused on the school's financial ties to slavery but also on the ways that faculty historically used religious language to justify it. At the time, experts said that confronting the theological underpinnings of slavery called for a "deep reckoning" not just about the past but also about how those ideas might influence today's institutions and theology's overarching role in contemporary public discourse. But what that reckoning should look like, in addition to some form of financial reparations, has largely been an open-ended question. How can schools, for example, quantify and repair harm caused by a bad ideology—and generations of students trained in it? Courageous transparency from these schools would be a first step, but for private schools like Georgetown and Brown Universities, canceling student loans for Black Americans could be another major step in the right direction. It would align with Jackson Lee's reparations proposal, a reminder of the promise made by General William T. Sherman in his 1865 Special Field Order No. 15. That decree—which focused on the redistribution of four hundred thousand acres of formerly Confederate-owned coastal land in South Carolina and Florida, subdivided into forty-acre plots, to former slaves—otherwise known as "40 acres and a Mule," was an early representation of reparations. But President Andrew Jackson, bowing to political pressure from Southern sympathizers, quickly overturned the order.

A LEGACY OF INEQUALITY

Advocates have long argued that the classification of the student debt crisis as just an "economic" problem that rests individually with the borrower totally overlooks the role of systemic and institutionalized racism, especially when it comes to the legacy of white supremacy directed toward African Americans in the United States. The very essence of the student debt crisis, they've rightly argued, is a story that is deeply rooted in historical injustice and one that has consistently rewarded the rich while disenfranchising countless others. The path to education both at the K–12 and higher education levels has been especially uneven for millions of Black people who descended from slaves, Jim Crow oppressors, and generations who experienced redlining and other systemic racial injustices for more than four hundred years. As a result of this widespread discrimination, too many Black and Brown students have found themselves excessively reliant on student loans due to their restricted access to familial money, thereby widening the socioeconomic gaps. For the activists who took up the cause as a civil rights issue, advocating for the cancellation of student loans is a form of restitution or reparations. For them, it's never been about "handouts" but about righting a historical wrong

Black Lives Matter (BLM), the organization that sprung up after the deaths of Trayvon Martin, Michael Brown, Eric Garner, Rekia Boyd, and others, included student debt forgiveness as part of their overall platform to address the racial wealth gap in the US. "We demand reparations for past and continuing harms," BLM asserted, adding that any form of reparations should also include "free access and open admissions to public community colleges and universities, technical education (technology, trade and agricultural), educational support programs, retroactive forgiveness of student loans, and support for lifetime learning programs."[6]

BLM's focus on education wasn't a coincidence but intentional, Ali Mir and Saadia Toor pointed out in their 2023 article titled "Racial Capitalism and Student Debt in the U.S." The authors noted that because of slavery, Black people were historically denied access to higher education, which closed its doors to them. It was not until 1837, with the founding of the nation's first HBCU—Cheyney University in Pennsylvania—that Black people had the opportunity to access higher education free from reprisal. "Racist public policies as well as de facto forms of racism have not only left the emancipatory potential of education unmet but have actually turned the project of higher education into a debt trap for African Americans," the authors wrote. "It is precisely because of the connection made by [W. E. B] Du Bois between education and Black emancipation, and the actual perversion of the promise of public education—both as the guarantor of social mobility and as the means for achieving racial equality—that the BLM movement seeks to draw our attention to the racial aspects of the current crisis of student debt."[7]

The data are clear on this issue. White families currently possess about eight times the amount of wealth as Black families, as Andre Perry and Carl Romer noted in their article "Student Debt Cancellation Should Consider Wealth."[8] The authors pointed out that "there is a significant wealth disparity between Black and non-Black people at every age group, and Black people are not building wealth at the same pace as their non-Black peers, particularly in their prime working ages." The authors noted that Black households' economic position is often precarious, and defaulting can actively jeopardize their financial health. Yet when we talk about student debt cancellation, rarely is that conversation centered on the experiences of Black Americans—missing a significant part of the problem.[9]

Given this important point, the enduring discussion about student debt relief is incomplete without a contextual examination of American history and how slavery impacted the financial outcomes for so many Black Americans and led to wealth inequality. Even the college admissions process—and the age-old debate over who gets in and who does not—must be radically reframed to consider the myriad ways that racism and discrimination has historically locked Black Americans out of accessing higher education for many years. Thankfully, HBCUs were created to help remedy this gross inequity and has educated millions of Black Americans for almost two hundred years. This is why student debt relief activists like McMillan have called for a form of reparations to be provided to Black Americans for the legacy of slavery and have also called for free college tuition and no loans for Black Americans. That is why they marched back in August 2023 to raise their voices too. Repayment in the form of student debt forgiveness, they declared, would send a powerful message: America is willing to make amends for its past to ensure that those who seek knowledge are not subjected to years of financial servitude and that progress depends on freeing those who are oppressed of their yokes. To achieve their end goal, they would not only turn to the activists of the 1960s for guidance, but they would also carefully study the legislative victories of the past for inspiration as they charted their path forward.

4 | FACTORS DRIVING THE STUDENT DEBT CRISIS

I spent my career studying why so many hardworking middle-class families were going broke. I discovered that they weren't reckless or irresponsible—they were being squeezed by an economy that forced them to take on more debt to cling to their place in America's middle class. Student debt is no different: for decades, students have worked hard and played by the rules. They took on loans on the promise that a college education would justify their debt and provide a ticket to the middle class. But our country's experiment with debt-financed education went terribly wrong: instead of getting ahead, millions of student loan borrowers are barely treading water.

Massachusetts Senator Elizabeth Warren,
speaking to reporters in 2021

How did the United States get to the point where the total student loan debt has surpassed $1.7 trillion? It's a question that I have been thinking about quite often as I travel throughout the nation to report and write about higher education issues. Time and time again, experts have told me that one of the primary drivers of the student debt crisis is the dramatic increase in college tuition and fees over the past few decades. After adjusting for inflation, the average cost of attending a four-year college has more than doubled since the 1980s. Several other factors have contributed to this rise, including reduced state funding for public universities, increased administrative costs, expansion of campus facilities and amenities, and growth in high-paying administrative positions.

To understand the current student debt crisis, it's first important that we understand the historical evolution of higher education funding in the United States. The landscape of college financing has undergone dramatic changes over the past century, shifting from a primarily public-funded model to one increasingly reliant on individual student debt. As a result, the student debt crisis in the United States is the result of a complex interplay of historical trends, policy decisions, economic factors, and societal shifts.

THE GI BILL AND POSTWAR EXPANSION

The modern era of higher education in America began in earnest with the Servicemen's Readjustment Act of 1944, commonly known as the GI Bill. This landmark legislation provided returning World War II veterans with funds for college education, vocational training, and low-cost mortgages. The GI Bill not only expanded access to higher education but also set a precedent for government investment in human capital through education. In the decades following World War II, the United States experienced a significant expansion of its higher education system. The baby boom generation created unprecedented demand for college education, and state governments responded by heavily investing in public universities and community colleges. During this same period, tuition at public institutions was kept low, and state funding covered a substantial portion of operational costs.[1]

In the gritty and tough streets of Camden, New Jersey, where opportunity often seems as scarce as shade on a summer day, Robert Nixon found a path to higher education through an unexpected route: military service. Nixon's story is a testament to the transformative power of the GI Bill, a piece of legislation that has opened doors for millions of veterans since its inception. Nixon joined the military straight out of high school in the late 1970s. Like many young people from working-class backgrounds, he saw the armed forces as a way to serve his country and gain valuable life skills. What he didn't realize at the time was that his service would also pave the way for his academic future. "I didn't have to choose between the military and college," Nixon told me, his eyes bright with the memory. "I was able to do both."[2]

This ability to pursue both paths has been the cornerstone of the GI Bill's success. Originally designed to help World War II veterans reintegrate into civilian life, the bill has evolved over the decades to continue supporting service members in their post-military endeavors. For Nixon, the journey from military service to college campus wasn't immediate. After completing his service, he returned to Camden and worked various jobs to support himself and his family. But the dream of higher education lingered, a quiet but persistent whisper in the back of his mind. It wasn't until the 1980s that Nixon decided to act on that dream. Armed with the benefits provided by the GI Bill, he enrolled at Rutgers University, New Jersey's flagship public institution. The contrast between the structured environment of military life and the open, intellectually stimulating atmosphere of a university campus was stark, but Nixon enthusiastically embraced the change with characteristic determination. "Walking onto the Rutgers campus for the first time as a student, I felt like I was entering a whole new world," Nixon said. "It was intimidating, sure, but also incredibly exciting. I knew this was my chance to reshape my future."

The GI Bill covered Nixon's tuition and provided a monthly housing allowance, removing the financial barriers that might have otherwise made college attendance impossible. This support allowed Nixon to focus on his studies without the constant worry about how to pay for his education or support himself while in school. As a nontraditional student, he brought a unique perspective to his classes. His military experience and years in the workforce gave him a level of maturity and real-world understanding that enriched classroom discussions and group projects. Professors, he said, often praised his work ethic and dedication, traits that he honed during his years of military service. "The discipline I learned in the military served me well at Rutgers," he said. "I approached my studies with the same commitment I had given to my service. Failure simply wasn't an option."

Nixon's journey wasn't without challenges. Balancing academic responsibilities with family obligations tested his resolve on many occasions. There were late nights of studying after putting his children to bed, early mornings rushing to make it to class on time, and weekends spent in the library instead of relaxing at home. But the promise of a better future, made possible by the GI Bill, kept him going. In 1985, Nixon's perseverance paid off. He walked across the stage at Rutgers' commencement ceremony, diploma in hand, a proud graduate with a degree in accounting. The moment was a triumph not just for him but also for his entire family and community. "Graduating from college was one of the proudest moments of my life," he said, his voice thick with emotion. "I knew I was setting an example for my kids, showing them that it's never too late to pursue your dreams." Today, Nixon is a successful business owner, using the skills he learned in college to contribute to his community's economic revitalization. He frequently speaks to local youth about the importance of education and the opportunities provided by military service. "The GI Bill gave me a second chance at education," he said. "It's not just about the degree, though that's important. It's about the doors that open when you have that education, the confidence you gain, and the example you set for others."

THE HIGHER EDUCATION ACT OF 1965

The passage of the Higher Education Act of 1965 (HEA), part of President Lyndon B. Johnson's Great Society program, established federal scholarships, low-interest loans, and work-study programs, further expanding access to higher education for middle- and lower-income students. The act created the foundation for many of the federal student aid programs that exist today, including Pell Grants and federally guaranteed student loans. Beginning in the 1970s and accelerating in the 1980s under Republican leadership, an ideological shift began to take place in how higher education was viewed and funded. The notion of education as a public good gave way to the idea of education as a private investment. This shift was accompanied by a gradual reduction in state funding for public universities, placing a greater financial burden on individual students and their families.

RISING COSTS OF COLLEGE TUITION

At the same time, college tuition started to rise. This increase in costs has far outpaced inflation and wage growth, making college increasingly unaffordable without taking on substantial debt. According to data from the College Board, between 1990 and 2020, the average tuition and fees at public four-year institutions increased by 361 percent (adjusted for inflation). Private nonprofit four-year institutions saw an increase of 258 percent (adjusted for inflation). These increases have been particularly pronounced since the early 2000s. For example, in-state tuition and fees at public four-year institutions increased by 212 percent between 2002 and 2022, far outpacing the 53 percent increase in the Consumer Price Index during the same period.[3]

Several factors have contributed to the rapid rise in college tuition. As state governments have faced budget constraints and competing priorities, funding for higher education is often the first to be cut. To make up for the lost revenue, public universities have responded by raising tuition. Between 2008 and 2018, state funding for public two- and four-year colleges decreased by $6.6 billion after adjusting for inflation. In 1988, public colleges received an average of $8,489 per student in state funding. By 2018, this had fallen to $7,853 (in 2018 dollars). These funding cuts have forced public institutions to rely more heavily on tuition revenue, shifting costs to students and their families. In a race to increase competition and attract more students, colleges have invested heavily in state-of-the-art facilities, luxury dormitories, and other amenities. These costs, in turn, are often passed on to students. The integration of advanced technology in classrooms and research facilities has also driven up operational expenses for universities.

The availability of federal financial aid, some experts have argued, may have paradoxically enabled colleges to raise tuition, as they know students have access to more borrowed money (this is known as the Bennett hypothesis).[4] Government policies at both the federal and state levels have played a crucial role in shaping the current student debt landscape. While many of these policies were intended to expand access to higher education, they have had unintended consequences that have contributed to the debt crisis. Over time, federal aid has shifted from a grant-based system to one heavily reliant on loans. In 1980, Pell Grants covered 77 percent of the cost of attending a four-year public university. By 2020, they covered only 28 percent. The introduction and expansion of programs like PLUS loans (which allow parents to borrow on behalf of their children) and unsubsidized Stafford loans have increased the availability of credit for education but also facilitated higher levels of borrowing.[5] The 2005 Bankruptcy Abuse Prevention and Consumer Protection Act has made it virtually impossible to discharge student loans in bankruptcy, removing an important safety net for borrowers and potentially encouraging riskier lending practices.[6]

Despite these rising costs, the economic value of a US college degree has remained high. The wage premium for college graduates (the difference in earnings between those with a college degree and those with only a high school diploma) has grown substantially since the 1980s. This has created strong incentives for individuals to pursue higher education, even at the cost of taking on significant debt. As more people have obtained college degrees, many jobs that previously did not require a degree have started to list it as a prerequisite. This phenomenon, known as "credential inflation,"[7] has pushed more individuals to pursue higher education simply to remain competitive in the job market. The shift toward a knowledge-based economy and the decline of manufacturing jobs have increased the importance of higher education for career success. Many high-paying jobs in growing sectors like technology, health care, and finance require advanced degrees, driving more people to pursue a college degree. There has also been a growing cultural expectation in the United States that attending college is a necessary step for success and upward mobility. This societal pressure has led some individuals to pursue higher education regardless of the cost, interests, or personal career goals.

STAGNANT WAGES AND ECONOMIC FACTORS

While the costs associated with accessing a higher education have skyrocketed, wages for most Americans have remained relatively stagnant, only further exacerbating the student debt crisis. This economic reality has made it increasingly difficult for individuals to afford college without borrowing and to repay their loans after graduation. Despite overall economic growth, wages for most American workers have seen little increase since the 1970s. Between 1979 and 2019, median hourly wages grew by just 14 percent after adjusting for inflation. In contrast, during this same period, productivity increased by about 70 percent.[8] The disconnect between productivity growth and wage growth has meant that even as the economy has wildly expanded, the average worker has not seen proportional gains in their earning power. At the same time, the top 1 percent of earners in the US saw their wages grow by 158 percent between 1979 and 2019. In contrast, wages for the bottom 90 percent grew by only

24 percent over the same period.[9] This growing disparity has meant that while a small segment of the population can easily afford rising education costs, the vast majority find themselves increasingly squeezed. The combination of stagnant wages and rising education costs has led to an increased reliance on student loans to finance education; greater difficulty in repaying loans after graduation; a higher debt-to-income ratio for recent graduates; and delayed major life milestones such as homeownership, marriage, and starting a family.

Equally concerning is the rise of predatory lending practices, particularly in the private student loan market. These discriminatory practices have trapped many borrowers into cycles of debt that are difficult, if not impossible, to escape. Some private lenders and for-profit colleges have engaged in aggressive marketing tactics to encourage students to take out loans. These tactics have often included misleading information about loan terms and repayment options, pressuring individuals to make quick decisions without fully understanding the implications and targeting vulnerable populations, including first-generation college students and low-income and minoritized individuals. Additionally, many of these private student loans also come with variable interest rates, which can increase significantly over time. This has led to the ballooning of loan balances that borrowers have struggled to repay. Unlike federal student loans, private student loans often lack important consumer protections such as income-driven repayment plans, loan forgiveness options, and deferment and forbearance options in cases of economic hardship. Many private lenders also require cosigners for student loans, often parents or other relatives. This practice can trap multiple generations in debt if the student is unable to repay the loan.

PREDATORY LENDING

In the spring of 2015, Jayson Albert's educational aspirations came crashing down around him. The Milwaukee resident was one of approximately sixteen thousand students left adrift when Corinthian Colleges, a for-profit institution, abruptly shut down all its remaining twenty-eight ground campuses. This closure came less than two weeks after the US Department of Education announced a $30 million fine against the institution for misrepresentation.

Albert, like many of his fellow students, found himself in a precarious position. "I didn't even know what predatory lending was," he recalled, "but I was a victim of it."[10] The realization that he had lost thousands of dollars pursuing what he now understood to be a worthless degree was a bitter pill to swallow. Corinthian Colleges' closure was the culmination of years of scrutiny and allegations of fraudulent practices. The for-profit college chain had been accused of falsifying job placement rates, misleading students about the transferability of credits, and engaging in aggressive and deceptive marketing tactics. For students like Albert, the collapse of Corinthian Colleges meant more than just the end of their current educational path—it represented a significant financial setback and a blow to their future prospects. "I had to start over again in my academic journey," he said. "It felt like all the time and money I'd invested had gone down the drain."

The closure of Corinthian Colleges brought to light the broader issues plaguing the for-profit college industry. Many students found themselves saddled with substantial debt for degrees that held little value in the job market. The predatory nature of the loans offered by these institutions often trapped students in cycles of debt with little hope of reprieve.

For years, Albert and thousands of others like him struggled under the weight of their student loans, uncertain if they would ever see relief. But in June 2022, a ray of hope emerged. The US Department of Education announced a landmark decision: it would discharge all remaining federal student loans borrowed to attend any campus owned or operated by Corinthian Colleges Inc. from its founding in 1995 through to its closure in April 2015. This sweeping action would result in 560,000 borrowers receiving $5.8 billion in full loan discharges.

For Albert, the news was almost too good to believe. "When I first read the announcement, I had to pinch myself," he said. "It felt like a weight was being lifted off my shoulders." The department's decision was unprecedented in its scope. Not only would it cover borrowers who had applied for borrower defense discharge, but it would also extend to those who had not yet applied. These borrowers would have their Corinthian loans discharged without any additional action on their part.

This action represented the largest single loan discharge in the department's history, highlighting the Biden administration's commitment to addressing the student debt crisis, particularly for those most adversely affected by predatory practices in higher education. "This targeted relief is part of our effort to ensure that all borrowers who've been harmed by their institutions get the discharges they're entitled to," a Department of Education spokesperson said at the time. "It's about making things right for the students who were wronged."[11]

For Albert, this decision meant more than just financial relief—it represented a chance at a fresh start. "Knowing that this debt won't be hanging over my head anymore, I feel like I can finally move forward," he said. "I can think about going back to school, about building a career, without this constant worry about how I'll pay off these loans."

The Corinthian Colleges loan discharge was part of a broader effort by the Biden administration to address student debt. While the road ahead may still hold challenges, for Jayson Albert and hundreds of thousands of former Corinthian students, the future looks considerably brighter. "Do your research. Ask questions. And remember, if something seems too good to be true, it probably is," Albert said.

The Corinthian Colleges case underscores a broader truth about the complexities and potential pitfalls of the modern higher education landscape. For students like Albert, the loan discharge represented not just financial relief but also a restored faith in the power of education to transform lives—when delivered with integrity and genuine commitment to student success.

THE CHALLENGE OF REPAYMENT

The 2008 financial crisis and the subsequent Great Recession had a profound impact on America's student debt crisis, exacerbating many of the trends that were already in motion. The recession led to severe budget shortfalls in many states, resulting in deep cuts to higher education funding. Between 2008 and 2017, state spending on public colleges decreased by 28 percent per student, adjusted for inflation.[12] These cuts forced public institutions to raise tuition even more rapidly to make up for lost funding. The 2008 financial crisis also wiped out significant wealth for many American families. The median household wealth fell by 39 percent between 2007 and 2010.[13] This loss of wealth meant that many families had fewer resources to contribute to their children's education, increasing reliance on student loans. The recession created a challenging job market for graduates. The unemployment rate for recent college graduates peaked at 7.1 percent in 2011.[14] Many graduates were forced to take lower-paying jobs or jobs outside their field of study. This made it more difficult for many borrowers to keep up with loan payments, leading to higher default rates.

All these factors created a perfect storm that made student debt repayment particularly difficult for many borrowers. In addition, the federal student loan repayment system is notoriously complex, with multiple repayment plans and forgiveness options. This complexity has led to borrower confusion about the best repayment strategy, difficulty navigating administrative processes, and missed opportunities for more favorable repayment terms. In addition, we have witnessed a series of problems across the years with student loan servicers, the companies that manage loan repayment. They have been criticized for misapplying payments, providing inaccurate or incomplete information about repayment options, and failing to properly process applications for income-driven repayment plans. In addition, many borrowers find themselves in situations where their payments are not enough to cover accruing interest, leading to negative amortization. This occurs when the loan balance grows over time despite regular payments. It can be particularly problematic in income-driven repayment plans where payments are capped based on income. Student loan default has severely hurt millions of borrowers, damaged credit scores, led to wage garnishment, and deemed a borrower ineligible for additional federal student aid. The default rate on federal student loans within three years of entering repayment was 9.7 percent for the 2017 cohort, highlighting the scale and magnitude of this issue.[15]

In the quiet suburbs of Indianapolis, Pete Benson, forty-four, sat at his kitchen table, a stack of unopened bills beside him. His eyes, tired and worried, scanned yet another rejection letter from a potential landlord. This scene, unfortunately, has become all too familiar for Benson since he defaulted on his student loans in 2018. "I never thought I'd be in this position," Benson told me, his voice tinged with frustration and regret. "I did everything I was supposed to do—went to college, got a decent job. But when the rug got pulled out from under me, it all came crashing down."[16]

Benson's story serves as a reminder of how quickly financial stability can unravel and how the consequences of student loan default can ripple through every aspect of a person's life. In 2018, Benson was working as a marketing manager for a midsize company. He had been steadily paying off his student loans for years, chipping away at the debt he'd accrued while earning his bachelor's degree. But when the company underwent a major restructuring, Benson found himself among the many employees laid off. "At first, I thought I'd find another job quickly," he said. "I had experience, a good track record. But the weeks turned into months, and suddenly keeping up with the student loan payments became impossible." As his savings dwindled and job prospects remained slim, Benson made the difficult decision to prioritize immediate needs—food, utilities, and housing—over his student loan payments. It wasn't long before he received notice that his loans were in default.

The impact was swift and far-reaching. Benson's once-solid credit score plummeted, closing doors he hadn't even realized existed. "It's like dominoes," he explained. "One thing falls, and suddenly everything else is tumbling down too." When his old car finally gave out, Benson found himself unable to secure a loan for a new one. "I never thought I'd miss having a car payment," he said. "But when you can't even get approved for that, you realize how much you've lost."

The challenges extended beyond transportation. Despite eventually finding a new job, albeit at a lower salary, Benson struggled to find a new place to live. Landlords, wary of his damaged credit, turned him down repeatedly. "It's humiliating," Benson told me. "Having to explain over and over why your credit is bad, why you can't provide a perfect rental history. It makes you feel like you're wearing a scarlet letter." The psychological toll of defaulting on his loans has been significant. Benson described feelings of shame and anxiety and a persistent sense of failure. "You start to internalize it," he said. "You think, 'Maybe I don't deserve a nice apartment. Maybe I don't deserve a reliable car.' It's a dark place to be in." Benson's story is not unique. According to recent statistics, over one million borrowers default on their student loans each year. The reasons vary—job loss, medical emergencies, or simply an inability to keep up with high monthly payments. But the consequences are often similarly devastating.

Financial experts emphasize the importance of communication with loan servicers before reaching the point of default. For Benson, the path forward is unclear but not without hope. He's been working with a credit counselor to slowly rebuild his financial health. "It's a long road," he acknowledged, "but I'm determined to get back on track." He's also become an advocate for student loan reform, sharing his story with the hope of sparking change. "The system is broken," he said. "Education is supposed to open doors, not slam them shut. We need to find a better way."

As Benson returned to his stack of bills, his resolve was clear. He's been knocked down, but he said that he refuses to stay on the ground. In his struggle, we see the face of a crisis affecting millions—a crisis that demands our attention and, more importantly, our action.

DISPARITIES

As we have already explored throughout this book, the student debt crisis has not affected all groups equally. Various demographic and societal factors have led to disparities in who bears the heaviest burden of student debt. Black students, for example, are more likely to take on student debt and in larger amounts. Four years after graduation, Black graduates owe an average of $52,726, compared to $28,006 for white graduates. These disparities are rooted in historical wealth inequality and ongoing systemic barriers.[17]

First-generation college students often face unique challenges, including a lack of information about navigating the complex world of college financing. They are more likely to come from lower-income backgrounds, necessitating higher borrowing, and may face additional pressures to support their families financially after graduation. While women are more likely to attend college, they hold about two-thirds of all student debt in the US.[18] The gender pay gap means women often have more difficulty repaying their loans.

In the fall of 1994, Megan Peterman stepped onto her college campus with a mix of excitement and trepidation. As a first-generation student, she was breaking new ground for her family, but she was also navigating uncharted waters. She didn't realize that she was about to embark on a financial journey that would impact her life for decades to come. "I felt like I was in a whole new world," she remembered. "Everything was new and exciting, but also overwhelming. I had no idea how to manage my finances."[19]

Peterman's experience was not unique. In the mid-1990s, college campuses across the United States were awash with credit card companies aggressively marketing to students. For many young adults, these shiny pieces of plastic represented a first taste of financial independence and a dangerous temptation. "They were everywhere," Peterman said, shaking her head. "Tables set up in the student union, flyers in our mailboxes, even representatives at campus events. It seemed like everyone was telling us to sign up."

Caught up in the excitement and lacking financial guidance, Peterman applied for not one but three credit cards: a Mastercard, an American Express, and a Discover card. To her surprise and delight, she was approved for all of them. "It felt like free money," she said. "I had no concept of interest rates or minimum payments. I just saw it as a way to buy things I couldn't otherwise afford."

What Peterman didn't fully grasp was that her work-study job at the library, which paid $6.75 an hour, was nowhere near enough to cover the expenses she was racking up on her credit cards. New clothes, meals out with friends, concert tickets—the charges added up quickly. "I was working about ten hours a week," she remembered. "In my mind, I thought that would be enough to cover everything. I didn't understand how quickly interest could accumulate."

As the semester wore on, Peterman found herself juggling minimum payments, often paying one card with another. The stress began to mount, but she felt too embarrassed to ask for help. "There was a lot of shame involved," she said. "I felt like I should have known better, even though no one had ever taught me about managing credit."

By the end of her first year, Peterman's financial situation had spiraled out of control. One by one, her credit cards were maxed out and then shut down. Her once-pristine credit score was in ruins. "It was devastating," Peterman recalled. "I went from feeling like an adult with financial freedom to realizing I'd made a huge mess that I had no idea how to clean up." The consequences of Peterman's credit card debt extended far beyond her college years. After graduation, she struggled to rent apartments and secure loans, and she even faced challenges in job hunting as some employers ran credit checks. "I had no idea how far-reaching the impact would be," she said. "It affected every aspect of my life."

Now, some thirty years later, Peterman is still working to recover from those early financial missteps. She's worked with credit counselors, diligently paid off old debts, and slowly rebuilt her credit score. But the journey has been long and challenging. "It's literally taken decades to undo the damage of those few years in college," Peterman said. "I've had to be incredibly disciplined and patient." In the years since her experience, regulations have been put in place to limit credit card marketing on college campuses, but the broader issue of financial education for young adults remains a concern. "I wish someone had sat me down and explained how credit works before I ever set foot on campus," she said. "It would have changed the course of my life."

Peterman now has two children in high school who will be headed off to college soon. "Knowledge is power," she said. "I've been teaching them about managing money and credit before they're faced with these kinds of decisions. I don't want them to make the same mistakes that I made."

"I can't change my past," she said, "but if my story can save my kids and maybe help others, then something good will have come from my experience."

Older and nontraditional students, part-time students, and those with dependents are sometimes ignored when it comes to discussions about the student debt crisis. But they often have other financial obligations that make it difficult to afford education without borrowing. In addition, they often take longer to complete their degrees, accruing more debt in the process, and often encounter more difficulty finding high-paying jobs after graduation due to age discrimination or family responsibilities.

A GLOBAL COMPARISON

The United States lags far behind other countries when it comes to the affordability of higher education. Germany, for example, abolished tuition fees for undergraduate students at public universities in 2014. Higher education is primarily funded through taxation.[20] Sweden provides free tuition for citizens and charges minimal fees for non-EU students. The government also offers generous grants and low-interest loans for living expenses.[21] In 1998, the United Kingdom introduced tuition fees and has since increased them. However, the UK uses an income-contingent repayment system where graduates begin repaying loans only when they earn above a certain threshold.[22] While

Canada has a system more similar to that of the US, the overall tuition costs are much lower than in the US and the Canadian government provides more grants and interest-free periods on loans.[23] In Australia, students can defer payment of tuition through government loans and repayment is income contingent, with graduates paying a percentage of their income once they reach a certain earnings threshold. Debts are indexed to inflation but do not accrue real interest.[24] These international examples, while not without their own challenges, do demonstrate that the US student debt crisis is not an inevitable outcome of providing higher education.

5 | UNRAVELING THE HIGHER EDUCATION ACT OF 1965

Here the seeds were planted from which grew my firm conviction that for the individual, education is the path to achievement and fulfillment; for the nation, it is a path to a society that is not only free but civilized; and for the world, it is the path to peace—for it is education that places reason over force.

President Lyndon B. Johnson, in a
speech upon signing the HEA

When President Joe Biden finally got around to focusing on student debt more than a year after he took office, he argued that his proposal would spread well beyond individual bank accounts and transform entire communities across the nation, breathing new life into a beleaguered economy. But every proposition must meet its judgment in the vast halls of American governance, and the US Supreme Court replied with a stinging defeat. The court, under the direction of Chief Justice John Roberts, examined the constitutional foundations of Biden's recommendations and wondered aloud if the executive branch of government could in fact use its authority to provide such comfort without going over-board. The court, in a six to three opinion, resoundingly struck down Biden's proposal in a decision symbolic of the frequently divided nature of contemporary American politics. The court ruled that Biden's proposed program, with such an enormous impact, went beyond the power of the US Department of Education and needed approval from Congress.

REACTIONS TO *BIDEN V. NEBRASKA*

The ruling should not have come as a total surprise to political observers. Just months earlier, commentators and legal experts prophesized that the plan was in serious trouble. When the high court's decision was finally made public, it was celebrated by conservatives from coast to coast. They argued that the effort was blatantly unfair from the start and had been designed to privilege some over others. The Biden administration disagreed. In February 2023, it argued that the forgiveness program was in fact permissible under the Higher Education Relief Opportunities for Students (HEROES) Act of 2003, which in the event of a national emergency, gave the secretary of education the power to "waive or modify" provisions of the HEA, which governs federal student aid. The emergency, it said, was the COVID-19 pandemic. But in his majority opinion, Chief Justice Roberts said that widespread loan forgiveness was unconstitutional. "The Secretary's plan has 'modified' the cited provisions only in the same sense that 'the French Revolution "modified" the status of the French nobility'—it has abolished them and supplanted them with a new regime entirely,"[1] Roberts wrote in the scathing opinion. Biden's debt relief program, Roberts opined, could not be justified as a "waiver," because it added new and different provisions to the law, such as the amounts that would be forgiven and the eligibility requirements. The administration's actions, the chief justice argued, were less of a waiver and more of a wholesale rewriting of the law that needed the approval of Congress. With Republicans squarely in control of the US House of Representatives in 2023, that scenario was highly unlikely. "What the Secretary has actually done is draft a new section of the Education Act from scratch by 'waiving' provisions root and branch and then filling the empty space with radically new text,"[2] Roberts wrote. He concluded that Congress would be the appropriate body to enact a mass debt cancellation and that it would not have intended for such a power to fall to the secretary of education, an affirmation of the so-called major questions doctrine, in which the court has historically required "clear Congressional authorization" for action on important issues of economic or political significance. As part of its sweeping decision, the court's majority also ruled that the state of Missouri, which sued on behalf of a group of six other states that claimed the debt relief program would have damaged them economically, had standing to bring the case, meaning that it had suffered a clear, direct injury from the proposed debt relief policy. The state had argued that if Biden's student relief program had proceeded, the Missouri Higher Education Loan Authority (MOHELA), a nonprofit government corporation, would have greatly suffered decreased revenues and would have been unable to make mandatory payments into a state fund. The court ruled that although MOHELA was distinct from the state itself, Missouri could still sue to remedy harm involving the nonprofit.

In a dissent that was joined by the court's other two liberal justices, Justice Elena Kagan, who served as the dean of Harvard Law School before she was appointed to the Supreme Court by

President Obama, argued that the court had dramatically overstepped its bounds by getting involved in an executive branch decision. "The Court is supposed to stick to its business—to decide only cases and controversies, and to stay away from making this Nation's policy about subjects like student-loan relief," Kagan wrote. She argued that Congress had chosen to delegate authority to the secretary of education to respond to emergencies and that the student loan forgiveness program was within the power that had been delegated. "That authority kicks in only under exceptional conditions," wrote Kagan. "But when it kicks in, the Secretary can take exceptional measures."[3]

In an afternoon speech from the White House hours after the court handed down its ruling, a somber-looking Biden acknowledged that he had been defeated during round one of the battle but vowed to fight on. He announced a plan to offer debt relief through an alternate source of authority: the HEA itself. He said that a line in that landmark legislation gave the secretary of education the power to "modify" and to "compromise, waive, or release" claims against borrowers without a precondition like a national emergency.[4]

But how, so many Americans skeptically wondered, could Biden be successful with this alternative pathway? With the 2024 presidential election on the horizon, some even wondered if his administration had the willpower and the resolve to continue the fight on. Higher education scholars were skeptical too. "The tone of the opinion and the reasoning suggest that the conservative supermajority would oppose an administration effort to do the same thing relying on a different law," remarked Jonathan Glater, a professor at the University of California, Berkeley. "I don't know what Congress could have written that would persuade the conservative justices in the majority that the Department has the authority to engage in cancellation."[5] For his part, Biden also announced plans at that press conference to create a "12-month on-ramp" program for borrowers that would temporarily remove the threat of default for those who missed initial payments. "The on-ramp to repayment will help borrowers avoid the harshest consequences of missed, partial, or late payments like negative credit reports and having loans referred to collection agencies," said his secretary of education, Miguel A. Cardona.[6]

The court's decision was, not surprisingly, hailed as a victory by Republicans, including several of the early 2024 presidential candidates. "Joe Biden's massive trillion-dollar student loan bailout subsidizes the education of elites on the backs of hardworking Americans, and it was an egregious violation of the Constitution for him to attempt to do so unilaterally with the stroke of the executive pen," wrote former Vice President Mike Pence on the social media platform called X, formerly known as Twitter. "I am pleased that the Court struck down the Radical Left's effort to use the money of taxpayers who played by the rules and repaid their debts in order to cancel the debt of bankers and lawyers in New York, San Francisco, and Washington, D.C."[7] Nikki Haley, the former South Carolina governor and United Nations ambassador who served in Donald Trump's administration, also piled on. "A president cannot just wave his hand and eliminate loans for students he favors, while leaving out all those who worked hard to pay back their loans or made other career choices," said Haley, who wound up challenging Trump for the Republican nomination but ultimately withdrew from the race and threw her support behind the president. "The Supreme Court was right to throw out Joe Biden's power grab."[8]

The ruling was also criticized on the other side of the political spectrum. The most vocal were higher education access groups. Sameer Gadkaree of The Institute for College Access & Success (TICAS) decried the ruling as a "significant blow to millions of borrowers, throwing their financial futures into uncertainty just as the pandemic payment pause is set to end. Policymakers must provide immediate help to those who were counting on this relief and support the administration's ongoing efforts to strengthen borrower protections and reform the repayment system going forward."[9] The Student Borrower Protection Center (SBPC), a nonprofit that aims to protect borrowers of student loans, struck an even angrier tone. "Today's decision is an absolute betrayal to 40 million student loan borrowers and their families counting on the court to uphold the law and move them closer to economic freedom," said Persis Yu, executive director of the SBPC, in a statement. "Caving to craven and naked political interests, this court relied on convoluted reasoning and distorted facts to allow these two politically contrived cases to deny desperately needed relief to tens of millions of low-income and working-class student loan borrowers."[10]

The Democrats on Capitol Hill decried the Republican-controlled court's ruling as "disappointing" and "cruel" and attempted to draw a connection between the justices receiving "lavish, six-figure gifts"—most notably Clarence Thomas, who reportedly accepted several trips from wealthy private donor Harlan Crow—and refusing to "help Americans saddled with student loan debt, instead siding with the powerful, big-monied interests."[11] Senate Majority Leader Chuck Schumer of New York pledged, "The fight will not end here. I call upon the administration to do everything in its power to deliver for millions of working- and middle-class Americans struggling with student loan debt."[12] Justin Draeger, former president and CEO of the National Association of Student Financial Aid Administrators, wondered whether the court's decision would ultimately lead to more-lasting fixes in the near future. "There's a real impasse on policy reform as it relates to student loans, so I don't know if this clears the way for us to think about bipartisan solutions," he said. "At some point, we need both Democrats and Republicans, Congress and the president, to be focusing on real reform to these loan programs so that today['s] and tomorrow's students don't have to carry so much loan debt."[13]

On September 1, 2024, after a three-year pause in payments because of the COVID-19 pandemic, the clock on student loan repayments suddenly started to tick again. Borrowers were put on notice that their regular loan payments would resume a month later. What the American people would quickly learn from the entire ordeal is that campaigning and governing are two vastly different realities. And campaign promises made by politicians don't immediately become reality. It's a practice that Joe Biden, a seasoned politician, understood, perhaps better than most, from his days as a powerful congressman, senator, and vice president.

BIDEN'S PROMISES

A year before the Supreme Court struck down Biden's student debt relief program, Senator Chuck Schumer had become a painful thorn in President Biden's side. The two had long enjoyed a cordial relationship, but the powerful Democrat who had been elevated to majority leader of the US Senate was getting annoyed by the slow pace of movement. There was no concrete proposal yet and Schumer decided to push the president at every turn to focus on the student debt crisis. It seemed that Biden's student debt proposal, outlined on the campaign trail, had suddenly fallen by the wayside. Schumer wanted Biden to go big on the student debt crisis and was certain that the American people would reward Democrats for their action. Biden, however, was not moved by the senator's strategy or his ongoing pressure. In fact, he had already rejected the idea of forgiving $50,000 in student debt, much to the chagrin of the progressive wing of his party. Doing so, he privately told his top aides, would be unfair to those Americans who successfully paid off their loans. Early on, he refused to stray far from those talking points in his public speeches either. "I will not make that happen," Biden said when questioned about the possibility of forgiving $50,000 in student debt during a CNN televised town hall meeting a month after taking office.[14] But Schumer remained relentless. He told Biden that if he canceled student debt, he would not be privileging rich, white kids who attended the nation's prestigious Ivy League schools but that his efforts, instead, would dramatically help most Americans who "are poor people and people of color."[15]

Determined to make an even stronger case to the commander in chief, Schumer buttonholed the president on Air Force One as the two traveled from Buffalo back to the nation's capital on a somber day in May 2022. They had made the short flight to upstate New York to visit with the families of ten victims who were racially targeted and gunned down by a white supremacist at a Tops supermarket. The shooting shocked the nation and the world. Payton Gendron stormed the popular grocery store on May 14, 2022, and opened fire. "White supremacy is a poison. It's a poison running through our body politic, and it's been allowed to fester and grow right in front of our eyes. No more," Biden said during remarks at a community center, with local leaders flanked by his sides. "We need to say as clearly and forcefully as we can that the ideology of white supremacy has no place in America."[16]

Biden's jam-packed agenda during his first year in office had been overly occupied with the ongoing COVID-19 pandemic and the spate of mass shootings that ravaged the nation, like the one that took him and the first lady, Dr. Jill Biden, to Buffalo to pay their respects to the families of victims who had become casualties in the ongoing fight against hatred and extremism. Committed he remained, however, to student debt relief and, with some cajoling from Schumer and others, came to believe that progress on student debt could become a signature part of his legislative legacy, like what Barack Obama did to make health care accessible and affordable.

Throughout the 2020 presidential campaign, Biden repeatedly sounded the alarm on the need to confront the very real financial hardships that Americans faced. As he traversed the nation, he told packed auditoriums that he understood their struggles and would move swiftly to deliver them from four years of inaction at the hands of President Donald J. Trump. "I'm going to make sure everyone gets $10,000 knocked off of their student debt," Biden said at the time.[17] On a roll, he refused to stop there. Instead, he proposed a series of other new financial incentives that he promised would remove barriers and open the doors to financial freedom, especially for the nation's most recent college graduates. He floated the idea, for instance, of providing a $15,000 credit that recent college graduates could use toward a down payment on their first home. "This is how people accumulate wealth," he proclaimed at a town hall meeting in Philadelphia. "This is how people get started. We have to recognize you and advance you. You are the future."[18]

During the 2020 Democratic primary, Biden faced an early barrage of criticism from his opponents and from some of the left-leaning Democrats within the halls of Congress. "[Ten thousand dollars of] means-tested forgiveness is just enough to anger the people against it and the people who need forgiveness the most," chided New York Congresswoman Alexandria Ocasio-Cortez, better known as AOC. "We can do better."[19] In a politically divided nation, with partisan lines clearly drawn, Biden had to proceed with caution. He was convinced that a push for a total elimination of all student loans was akin to calls by the progressives in his party to defund the police. Most Democrats, he believed, were far more centrist in their approach to these social and economic bread-and-butter issues. His political future, he warned aides, was at risk if he decided to cave in to pressure. He was not willing to take that risk.

Biden also had the benefit and advantage of memory. He remembered how tough it was to build consensus on the student debt relief issue during his time as vice president. In 2011, President Obama traveled to the Auraria Higher Education Campus in downtown Denver to generate support for a two-pronged student debt relief measure. The legislation had already received a green light from Congress, and Obama—gearing up for a run for reelection—appeared before thousands at a rally to promise that his administration would "speed up" an income-based repayment (IBR) provision of the law that would permit borrowers to cap their student loan payments at 10 percent of discretionary income—down from the previous 15 percent.

"We're going to make these changes work for students who are in college right now," Obama said to a steady applause. "We're going to put them into effect next year, because our economy needs it right now and your future could use a boost right now."[20] But not soon after Obama announced the provision, policy analysts quickly cautioned that the implementation of the Pay-As-You-Earn part of the measure was problematic because not all borrowers would benefit from the measure and, of those who were eligible, not all of them should be allowed to pursue the relief that was being offered anyhow. Obama's publicly touted student debt relief plan, critics charged, amounted to nothing more than a repayment program, not a student loan forgiveness program. In 2007, President George W. Bush signed the Public Service Loan Forgiveness (PSLF) program into law to encourage college graduates to pursue careers in service of the common good. Following the passage of that legislation, droves of social workers, educators, researchers, public-interest lawyers, nurses, and museum curators signed up to take advantage of the loan forgiveness program. Borrowers who worked for ten years in certain federal, state, local, or tribal government or nonprofit organizations became eligible to have their loans forgiven after they reached 120 qualifying monthly payments. That program remains in effect today.

Biden's three-part proposal, however, was different. In addition to the $20,000 in debt cancellation to Pell Grant recipients with loans held by the Department of Education, and up to $10,000 in debt cancellation to non–Pell Grant recipients, his proposal included several sweeping reforms to existing student loan programs. Even still, in the early days of the 2020 presidential campaign, his plan was attacked from both sides of the political aisle. Republicans criticized it and Democrats like Alexandria Ocasio-Cortez lamented that the measure did not go far enough. She called for a more radical and robust response and doubled down on her earlier criticisms of the part of the plan that called for the cancellation of $10,000 in federal student loan debt for only a select group of borrowers. Those restrictions, she said, were too modest and excluded millions of others who desperately needed relief.

On August 24, 2022, three months after Schumer aggressively lobbied Biden on Air Force One, the president finally unveiled his plan during a much-awaited speech held at the White House. It was historic. Millions of borrowers, he said, would finally be eligible to have $20,000 in student loans forgiven. In addition, he was ready to extend the payment freeze that had been in effect until the end of 2022 because of the global pandemic. "Education is a ticket to a better life. . . . but over time that ticket has become too expensive for too many Americans," Biden remarked.[21] "All this means that an entire generation is now saddled with unsustainable debt in exchange for an attempt, at least, at a college degree. The burden is so heavy that even if you graduate you may not have access to the middle-class life that the college degree once provided."[22]

Biden told the American people that borrowers who held loans with the Department of Education and made less than $125,000 a year were eligible for up to $20,000 in student loan forgiveness if they had received a Pell Grant. Individuals who made less than $125,000 a year but had not received a Pell Grant were eligible for $10,000 in loan forgiveness. He said that the administration's "targeted actions" were for families that needed the relief the most. That included, he said, "working and middle class people hit especially hard during the pandemic making under $125,000 a year."[23] He emphasized that 90 percent of the eligible beneficiaries who would benefit from this plan made under $75,000.

An astute political pragmatist, Biden was already prepared for the critiques and the backlash that would be directed his way. "I understand not everything I'm announcing is going to make everybody happy," he said matter-of-factly. "Some think it's too much—I find it interesting how some of my Republican friends who voted for those tax cuts think we shouldn't be helping these folks. Some think it's too little, but I believe my plan is responsible and fair. It focuses the benefit of middle-class and working families, it helps both current and future borrowers and it'll fix a badly broken system."[24]

In October 2022, the US Department of Education officially launched its application for student loan forgiveness, allowing an estimated twenty-seven million borrowers to seek debt relief via a website portal. More than sixteen million applicants promptly received approval from the Department of Education. Unlike the botched rollout of Obamacare in 2013, when the government website crashed at least three times, the rollout of the student debt relief program was remarkably seamless. Finally, borrowers thought they would suddenly get a reprieve from the grueling monthly loan payments that had a foothold on their biweekly and monthly earnings. But that would not be so—at least not yet. Almost immediately, lawsuits were filed by organizations, individuals, and state governments. Some argued that Biden's proposal conflicted with the PSLF program. There were other challenges, too, including a three-count complaint from the Brown County Taxpayers Association in Wisconsin. The organization, which claimed to be committed to "fiscal responsibility in government," alleged that Biden's plan violated the constitutional equal protection doctrine; the "defendants announced an explicit racial motivation" as justification for moving forward with efforts to stop the program. Their lawsuit charged that the plan was discriminatory in nature and would hurt whites.[25] But borrowers signed up anyway. The rollout, said Dominique Baker, a higher education scholar, conformed "to the best practices of what we would hope an application does for government benefits."[26] She added: "It's relatively short. It's all information that is generally at the person's fingertips, in their head already. The amount of time and energy that someone has to put into completing it has been reduced as much as possible."[27] Simple and accessible, Baker added, was certain to win the Biden administration widespread support. And it did. Commentators gave the administration high marks for the overall launch. "I was kind of expecting it to be pretty similar to [the Obamacare sign-up] but it was kind of the opposite," noted Melissa Larson, a borrower saddled with debt from her time at Macalester College. She completed the form on her phone. "It was shockingly easy. I was on Instagram or something and someone I follow posted a link to the application, so I went there. It took like two seconds. There was no crashing. My confirmation email came right away."[28]

Similarly, Ben Wisniewski, a borrower who accumulated debt from his time at the University of Hawaii law school, had an easy time when he used the beta version of the application. "I had zero problems with it," he said. "The form was mercifully short. I think I was able to fill it out in like 10 minutes even after paranoid double-checking. I think they did an A+ job."[29] The timing of the application's release was politically significant for several reasons, noted Robert Kelchen, head of the Department of Educational Leadership and Policy Studies at the University of Tennessee, Knoxville. "It's in advance of the midterm elections and it's in advance of some of the lawsuits that are coming up," he said at the time. "I think they [the Biden administration] would very much like to start forgiving debt before the midterms if courts allow them to do so." Added Kelchen, "It makes debt forgiveness more real, more salient, if people have filled out an application for it. If there is a successful lawsuit against debt forgiveness, the Biden administration is hoping that those borrowers will then go out and blame Republicans."[30]

Even before it was clear that Biden's program was in serious trouble, Larson's experience with the application gave her the confidence that she and others were well on their way to receiving financial relief. "The fact that it was easily accessible on a phone made me hopeful that everything's going to be smooth," she said. "I've noticed a lot of the people in communities that I follow on social have been posting about this a lot. I hope the ease makes it so everyone actually does it."[31]

But after the Supreme Court ruling halted any debt forgiveness, Larson and others were back in a wait-and-see posture. They were hopefully optimistic but realistic, too, as they readied themselves for an ultimate defeat and a return to their monthly student loans payments.

The only thing that could save them now was the HEA.

"NOT GIVING UP"

After the US Supreme Court struck down President Biden's student loan forgiveness program, a strident President Biden vowed that his administration would not give up the fight, swiftly announcing plans to offer debt relief under an alternative authority, the HEA. Unlike his initial plan, which was accomplished by executive order, his second effort required a somewhat complicated process known as negotiated rulemaking, in which stakeholders get a chance to negotiate potential regulations. That process started in July 2023, when the Department of Education convened a virtual public hearing to get feedback on loan forgiveness efforts. The information was designed to help the department ensure that as many perspectives as possible were included among the negotiators to help shape the eventual regulation. Under Secretary of Education James Kvaal kicked off the process when he touted the Biden administration's other recent efforts to relieve pressure on borrowers. The speed with which the hearing was arranged—less than three weeks after the Supreme Court's ruling—was remarkable and provided evidence of the administration's seriousness to find workarounds to the issue despite the high court ruling.

Most of those who argued for forgiveness during the public hearing were young borrowers, who spoke on behalf of themselves. One by one, they said that they had been given the message that higher education was the way to prosperity, only to find out that the rug had been yanked from under them when they were left with debts that they could not pay based on their wages. Several discussed having balances soar far past the amount that they initially borrowed. "They're leeching the blood from us," said one borrower named Lisa Jones. "It feels like I'm being punished."[32] John Smith, another debtor, compared his debt to an albatross around his neck mixed with indentured servitude. At that hearing, the borrowers were joined by representatives of pro-forgiveness organizations, including the Student Borrower Protection Center, the Debt Collective, and We The 45 Million, as well as outfits like the New York Legal Assistance Group, the Institute of Student Loan Advisors, and Rise. They argued that any new forgiveness effort should include all the borrowers who would have received relief from the initial plan, which would have forgiven $10,000 for those earning under $125,000 and $20,000 for Pell Grant recipients. Some argued that the new Biden plan should go even further, with suggestions that included forgiving $50,000 of debt and, from a few borrowers, forgiving all student debt. Several speakers said that Parent PLUS loans and graduate school loans should have been included in the plan as well. Others focused on the negotiated rulemaking process itself. Thomas Gokey, a debtor and organizer of the Debt Collective, made the case that the negotiating sessions over the rule should have taken place virtually, to make it easier for the public to engage and to reduce the chances of negotiators ganging up on and bullying each other. He said that it was important that all kinds of borrowers be on the committee, including women, borrowers of color, borrowers from HBCUs and other Minority-Serving Institutions (MSIs), borrowers who are in default, older borrowers, borrowers who don't have a degree, single-parent borrowers, borrowers with disabilities, and those who have paid off their loans.

Rep. Maxwell Frost, a Democrat from Florida and the first congressperson to be a member of Generation Z, took to the podium. Elected to the US House of Representatives at the age of twenty-five, Frost previously served as national organizing director for March for Our Lives, the student-led organization that spearheaded demonstrations in support of gun control legislation after the 2018 deadly shooting at the Marjory Stoneman Douglas High School in Parkland, Florida. He received national headlines after he was denied an apartment in Washington, DC, following his election to Congress. "Just applied to an apartment in DC where I told the guy that my credit was really bad. He said I'd be fine. Got denied, lost the apartment, and the application fee. This ain't meant for people who don't already have money," Frost tweeted about his ability to secure affordable housing in the nation's capital. "It's unfortunate. It's a known issue, especially amongst the more working-class members. It's definitely a problem," he said.[33]

At the hearing, Frost—who attended Valencia College in Orlando but dropped out before his senior year—said that student debt relief was one of the top issues that constituents had contacted him about in the months after he was elected. He urged the Biden administration to fight to keep the terms of the program as they were originally announced.

There were detractors too. Mark Chenoweth of the New Civil Liberties Alliance argued that any plan for broad debt relief using the HEA would be "pulling a wooly mammoth out of a statutory mousehole." He said that a vote of Congress would be required for debt forgiveness and noted that there would inevitably be people or organizations with the standing to sue over Biden's unilateral actions. Joining Chenoweth was Karen Harned of the Job Creators Network, who described the proposed relief as "just a band-aid" that wouldn't fix the underlying problem of skyrocketing tuition. "We're going to be back here in five, ten, fifteen years, doing this once again," she said.[34] Still, many of the advocates at that hearing held out hope that the Biden administration would act quickly. But they also knew that in the world of negotiated rulemaking, speed is relative. Once the hearing ended, the Department of Education pledged to figure out which kinds of stakeholders would be included in the negotiations before they issued the call for nominations, followed by a Notice of Proposed Rulemaking, public comment, and final revision of the obscure regulation.

THE HIGHER EDUCATION ACT OF 1965

The HEA stands as a landmark piece of legislation that fundamentally reshaped access to higher education in the country. Signed into law by President Lyndon B. Johnson as part of his Great Society domestic agenda, the HEA was designed to strengthen educational resources and provide financial assistance to students seeking postsecondary education. However, in the decades since its enactment, the landscape of higher education financing has changed dramatically, culminating in what can only be referred to as a national student debt crisis.

HEA was born, however, out of a period of significant social and economic change in the United States. Following World War II, there was a growing recognition of the importance of higher education in driving economic growth and maintaining global competitiveness. However, access to college remained limited for many Americans, particularly those from lower-income backgrounds. From its inception, the goals of HEA included strengthening the educational resources of colleges and universities, providing financial assistance for students in postsecondary and higher education, and expanding access to higher education for underrepresented groups.

The act established several important programs and initiatives to achieve these goals. Among them were the Educational

Opportunity Grants (now known as federal Pell Grants). These need-based grants were created to help low-income students access higher education without incurring debt. Unlike loans, these grants do not need to be repaid. The Guaranteed Student Loan Program (later known as the Federal Family Education Loan [FFEL] Program and Direct Loan Program) provides government guarantees for loans made by private lenders to students. This guarantee reduces the risk for lenders, making it easier for students to obtain loans for higher education. Finally, the Work-Study Program—an initiative that provides part-time jobs for undergraduate and graduate students with financial need, allowing them to earn money to help pay for their education expenses—falls under HEA. The passage of HEA marked a significant shift in federal policy, establishing the government's role in directly supporting individual students' pursuit of higher education. The philosophy underpinning these key provisions was that financial barriers should not prevent capable students from accessing a college education.

Since its inception in 1965, the HEA has undergone several reauthorizations and amendments, each shaping the landscape of student financial aid. For example, the reauthorization in 1972 established the Student Loan Marketing Association (Sallie Mae) to create a secondary market for student loans. The Basic Opportunity Grant (now called the Pell Grant) was also introduced. Twenty years later, in 1992, the reauthorization included some key provisions. Unsubsidized Stafford loans became available to all students regardless of financial need and loan limits were increased. In 1998, the reauthorization lowered interest rates on student loans and expanded loan forgiveness programs for teachers. The Higher Education Reconciliation Act of

2005 introduced Grad PLUS loans, allowing graduate students to borrow up to the full cost of attendance. The College Cost Reduction and Access Act of 2007 increased the Pell Grant maximum and introduced IBR and PSLF programs. The Health Care and Education Reconciliation Act of 2010 ended the FFEL Program, shifting to direct lending from the government.

These changes, while often intended to improve access and affordability, have also contributed to the increasing complexity of the student loan system and, in some cases, to rising levels of student debt. The expansion of federal student loan programs, coupled with rising college costs, has also led to a significant increase in student borrowing over the past few decades. In 1970, only about 15 percent of students borrowed money for college. By 2012, this figure had risen to nearly 70 percent. The total student loan debt in the US reached $1.75 trillion in 2024. This represents a more than 100 percent increase from 2010. In 2022, the average student loan debt for recent college graduates was approximately $30,000. For graduate students, this figure is significantly higher, often exceeding $100,000. As of 2024, about one in ten borrowers were in default on their federal student loans and many more are struggling with repayment, even if they are not technically in default.[35] This exponential growth in student debt has far-reaching implications for individuals, families, and the broader economy.

While the HEA played a significant role in shaping the current landscape, several other factors have contributed to the student debt crisis that we face today, most notably rising college costs, wage stagnation, increased college enrollment, extended time to degree completion, the rise of for-profit colleges, a complex and convoluted repayment process, and economic recessions. Tuition and fees at both public and private institutions have outpaced inflation, and state funding for public universities has dramatically decreased, shifting more costs to students. Despite rising education costs, wages for many college graduates have remained relatively flat, making it harder for graduates to repay their loans. More students are currently pursuing higher education, including those from lower-income backgrounds, and these individuals need to borrow to pay for the rising costs. Additionally, more and more students are taking longer to complete their degrees, accumulating more debt in the process. The rise of for-profit colleges like the University of Phoenix, for example, has done a good job at attracting students of color. But these institutions often have higher tuition and lower graduation rates, leading to higher debt and default rates. The variety of repayment plans and forgiveness programs has proven to be confusing for borrowers. The 2008 financial crisis and the global COVID-19 pandemic have made it much harder for many borrowers to repay their loans.

Some have argued that the HEA, while revolutionary in its approach to expanding access to higher education, has inadvertently contributed to the current student debt crisis by providing easy access to credit, through the guarantee of federal loans making credit readily available to students. Over time, the balance of federal aid has shifted from grants to loans, which has increased the debt burden on students, particularly those from lower-income backgrounds. Federal student loans do not consider credit history or the ability to repay, which can also lead to over-borrowing by some students, who take out additional funds to purchase vehicles or other technological devices that they cannot afford. Critics have charged that successive amendments to the HEA have created a complex system of loans, repayment plans, and forgiveness programs that has led to suboptimal borrowing and repayment decisions. Many borrowers are also unaware that changes to the HEA have made student loans very difficult to discharge in bankruptcy, leaving some borrowers with no way out of insurmountable debt. These skeptics have also charged that the HEA's focus on access did not initially include strong measures to hold institutions accountable for student outcomes and debt levels. While HEA's goal of expanding access to higher education has been largely successful, these unintended consequences have contributed significantly to the current crisis.

When President Johnson signed the HEA into law, he made a forceful argument that families "would finance college education for their children in the same way that they finance the purchase of a home."[36] But that kind of language—however well-intentioned—left out millions of Americans who never had the wherewithal financially to make that happen. Representing a profound metamorphosis within the American educational landscape, the legislation aimed to proliferate educational opportunities by providing financial assistance to a diverse array of students, breaking the chains of economic and societal barriers that had long stifled the aspirations of many. At its core, the act was infused with a transformative spirit and sought to provide a doorway to higher learning for individuals for whom such an endeavor was a distant mirage. This was not merely a fiscal realignment but a reconceptualization of the very fabric of societal and educational norms. Its provisions included increased federal funding to colleges, the provision of scholarships, and the establishment of a student loan program, illuminating paths to learning that had remained shadowed for far too long. For communities that were historically marginalized and economically disadvantaged, like

African Americans, the act eventually served as a beacon of hope and a promise of equitable access to the reservoirs of knowledge. Black people viewed this act as a gateway to empowerment and social mobility, enabling them to rewrite their narratives marred by historical subjugation and marginalization.

But beyond mere academic accessibility, the HEA also acted as an important catalyst, invoking a deeper examination of the hierarchical structures within educational institutions. It encouraged an interrogation of the hegemonic norms and propelled the drive toward a more inclusive and equitable academic environment. The HEA essentially asked Americans to fundamentally reconsider the essence of education, its role as a social equalizer, and its potential to dismantle entrenched paradigms of inequality and discrimination. Subsequent reauthorizations and amendments have aimed at refining its provisions, aligning them with the dynamic educational needs and societal contexts. Each amendment, however, broadly reflects the ongoing conversation about the role and reach of education in molding the destinies of individuals and the nation. It's important to note that the implementation and execution of the act has not been devoid of challenges and controversies. The ongoing quest for educational equity has long been fraught with complexities and conflicting interests. Debates surrounding the allocation and adequacy of funds, the ever-increasing burden of student loans, and the accessibility to quality education continue to echo in the hallways of policymaking chambers and academic forums.

6 | THE ARCHITECT OF THE PELL GRANT

The strength of the United States is not the gold at Fort Knox or the weapons of mass destruction that we have, but the sum total of the education and the character of our people.

Rhode Island Senator Claiborne Pell, in a speech delivered in 1996 upon his retirement

Six years after President Johnson signed the HEA, legislators in both chambers of Congress—the House of Representatives and the US Senate—were busy working hard to figure out how best to help poor and working-class students access college in ways that had previously been available to only the wealthy. Johnson had declared a "war on poverty" and part of his Great Society program included the creation of a wave of new social service initiatives designed to help the struggling poor. Despite widespread criticism by conservative politicians who were largely opposed to the escalation of these kinds of social programs, Johnson's efforts gained momentum throughout the late 1960s and into President Richard Nixon and Vice President Gerald Ford's administration of the early 1970s. The legislation gained additional support during Jimmy Carter's administration in the late 1970s and then faced an insurmountable backlash and severe fiscal cutbacks during the presidencies of Ronald Reagan and George H. W. Bush. However, remnants of what Johnson originally proposed still exist today in a variety of forms including Head Start, TRIO—which includes the Upward Bound program—and Job Corps, among a host of other important social service programs.

PELL'S VISION

On the education front, Claiborne de Borda Pell—the six-term Rhode Island senator who served from 1961 to 1997—rode into Congress with an ambitious advocacy agenda and a clear mandate. Within no time, he quickly emerged as an ardent supporter for low-income students and a man whose legacy would be defined by his work toward advancing access to college. Pell believed that a college education could serve as a vehicle to improve one's social standing within society. So impressive was his legislative record and stewardship that a federal grant that he helped to design to provide financial support to low-income undergraduate students was eventually renamed in his honor. He became the father of the Pell Grant.

Walk onto any college campus in America and you'll likely find Pell students. In the more than five decades since its existence, millions of students have accessed higher education through this subsidy. Unlike private or federally subsidized and unsubsidized loans, the Pell Grant does not have to be repaid. This legislative victory was perhaps the first outward demonstration of a nation's decision to codify a moral imperative to help ease the financial burden associated with the cost of paying for college.

On the surface, Pell seemed an unlikely character to take up the cause for the nation's poor and working-class students. He was born on November 22, 1918, into a world of privilege, old money, and political legacy. His father, Herbert Pell, served as a congressman from New York. Another five of Pell's family members also served in the US House or Senate, including his great-great-granduncle George Dallas, who was a senator from Pennsylvania in the 1830s and vice president under President James Polk in the 1840s.[1]

Claiborne Pell's own education was anything but ordinary. He attended the prestigious St. George's School in Newport, Rhode Island, before moving on to Princeton University. His time at Princeton was interrupted by World War II, during which he served in the Coast Guard and personally benefited from the GI Bill. He then went on to earn a master's degree in history at Columbia University and served in the US Foreign Service, where he held diplomatic posts in Europe before returning to Rhode Island in the 1950s.

These experiences, set against the backdrop of his family's fluctuating fortunes, instilled in Pell a unique perspective on the value and challenges of higher education. He witnessed first-hand the doors that a quality education could open, as well as the financial barriers that could prevent talented individuals from accessing those opportunities. Pell believed that everyone in America should have the opportunity to receive an education, regardless of wealth or ability. And if given the chance to advance themselves via education, Americans, he argued, would be able to not only better the lives of their families but to also advance the nation. In this regard, Pell was equally convinced that government—and the federal government in particular—had a central role to play in this process.

Following in the political footsteps of his father, the younger Pell quickly earned a national reputation for having progressive ideas, especially when it came to the arts and education. He put his ideas into practice when he authored landmark legislation that created the Basic Educational Opportunity Grant (BEOG), which was intended to create a "floor" for an eligible student's financial aid in an effort to help defray the costs of a postsecondary education. Pell believed "strongly that a good education could open infinite doors of opportunity, and he has transformed the lives of millions of young people who have been able to go to college because of the grant that rightly bears his name,"[2] said US Senator Edward M. Kennedy, in a statement issued in January 2009, shortly after Pell died after a long battle with Parkinson's disease at the age of ninety.

Pell's entry into politics came in 1960 when he was first elected to the United States Senate as a Democrat from Rhode Island. From the outset, he made education a cornerstone of his political agenda, arguing that education was not just a personal benefit but also a public good. Higher education, he opined, should be a right for all Americans, not a privilege reserved for the wealthy. He saw education as the great equalizer, capable of breaking cycles of poverty and opening opportunities for social advancement. In the context of the Cold War, Pell argued that an educated populace was essential for America's national security and technological supremacy.

These deep convictions drove Pell to become one of the Senate's most vocal and effective advocates for higher education. During his long tenure on Capitol Hill, he worked tirelessly to expand federal support for colleges and universities, to increase funding for research, and most importantly, to make college more affordable for students from low- and middle-income families. But his signature achievement in this arena was his role in working with the Johnson White House to craft and champion the HEA. As a member of the Senate Education Subcommittee, Pell was deeply involved in crafting the act. In addition to established federal scholarships for undergraduates (which would later evolve into Pell Grants), the act created a guaranteed student loan program, provided funding for college libraries and other educational resources, and established the National Teacher Corps.

THE BASIC EDUCATIONAL OPPORTUNITY GRANT

The impact of the HEA was immediate and far-reaching. In the years following its passage, college enrollment increased significantly, particularly among lower-income and minority students, making higher education a reality for millions of Americans who previously saw it as an unattainable dream. However, Pell recognized that while the act was a significant step forward, more could be done to ensure equal access to higher education. He continued to work on refining and expanding the federal government's role in supporting college students through the development of the BEOG. Building on the foundation laid by the HEA, Pell advocated for a more comprehensive and accessible form of federal student aid. His vision was a program that would provide grants, not loans, to students based on their financial need.

His persistence paid off. In 1972, the BEOG Program was created as part of the Education Amendments of 1972. This program would later become known as the Pell Grant program. The BEOG Program was revolutionary in several ways, most notably that it was need-based. Unlike other existing scholarships, the grants were awarded based solely on financial need, not academic merit. Students could also use the grants at any eligible institution, giving them more choice in their educational pursuits. Finally, the program was structured as an entitlement, meaning that all eligible students would receive grants rather than being subject to limited funding.

Senator Pell's approach to developing this program was characterized by his trademark pragmatism and bipartisanship. He worked across party lines, built strategic coalitions, and made compromises whenever it was necessary to ensure the program's passage. One of the key debates that surrounded the creation of the BEOG Program was whether to provide aid directly to students or to institutions. Pell argued strongly for student-centered aid, believing that this approach would empower students and promote competition among institutions to provide the best education at the most reasonable cost.

The senator's vision for the program was expansive. He saw it not just as a means of financial assistance but also as a way to democratize higher education and invest in the nation's future. In a speech supporting the program, Pell famously said, "The strength of the United States is not the gold at Fort Knox or the weapons of mass destruction that we have, but the sum total of the education and the character of our people."[3] The BEOG Program was implemented in the 1973–74 academic year. In its first year, the program provided grants to approximately 176,000 students. The maximum grant amount was $452, a significant sum at the time for many low-income students.[4]

Over the next few years, the program grew rapidly: during the 1974–75 academic year, there were 567,000 recipients; during the 1975–76 academic year, there were 1.2 million recipients; and during the 1976–77 academic year, the program served more than 1.9 million recipients. As the program expanded, it faced various challenges and underwent several modifications. For his part, Pell remained actively involved in overseeing its implementation and advocating for its expansion. At every turn, he fought tirelessly for increased funding, higher maximum grant amounts, and broader eligibility criteria. He saw the program as a vital investment in America's future, often arguing that the cost of the grants was far outweighed by the economic and social benefits of a more educated populace. Even after the Pell Grant program became established as a cornerstone of federal student aid, Pell's work was far from over. He recognized that the landscape of higher education was constantly evolving, and he worked to ensure that federal policy kept pace with these rapid changes. Over time, Pell advocated for extending grant eligibility to part-time students and those in vocational programs, recognizing the diverse needs of learners. He consistently pushed for higher appropriations for the program, arguing that grant amounts needed to keep pace with rising college costs. Pell supported initiatives to help students and families better understand their options for financing higher education. He recognized the growing importance of lifelong learning and worked to ensure that federal aid programs accommodated older students returning to education. And as student loan debt began to emerge as a significant issue, Pell advocated for measures to keep borrowing manageable and to provide relief for borrowers.

THE LEGACY OF PELL

When Pell's long Senate career ended in 1997, the program that bore his name had become an integral part of the American higher education system. The impact of Pell Grants on individual lives and on the nation has been profound. Millions of students who might otherwise have been unable to afford college have pursued higher education thanks to Pell Grants. The program has played a crucial role in increasing the racial and socioeconomic diversity of college campuses. By making college more accessible, Pell Grants have helped many individuals move up the economic ladder, breaking cycles of poverty. The program has also contributed to a more educated workforce, benefiting the overall economy, and has helped to solidify the idea that higher education should be accessible to all, regardless of financial background.

The impact of the Pell Grant program extends beyond just the numbers. Many colleges and universities have developed support programs specifically for Pell Grant recipients, recognizing the unique challenges these students may face. The program has served as a model for other need-based aid programs at both the state and institutional levels.

The emergence of the Pell Grant—perhaps more than any other federal financial subsidy—became the legislative linchpin for higher education. Yet the grant has received only small incremental increases throughout its fifty-year existence. Under President Bill Clinton's administration in 1993, the maximum amount awarded for Pell was $3,649. Ten years later, in 2003, the most that a student could receive was $5,046. Since 2003, the Pell Grant largely remained flat until President Biden decided in 2023 to increase the award amount to $7,395. That increase came amid calls from higher education advocacy groups like the United Negro College Fund (UNCF) and the Thurgood Marshall College Fund (TMCF), who urged Congress to pass legislation to double Pell. Ivory A. Toldson, a professor at Howard University who previously served as national director of education innovation and research at the NAACP agreed. "With the cost of living increasing every year, the Pell Grant often doesn't cover all of a student's expenses. In addition, the wealth gap continues to widen in the U.S., which means that there are more students who need help than ever before," said Toldson. "Inflation is a significant issue for students, as the cost of college continues to rise faster than the rate of inflation. A Pell Grant increase can help to ensure that these costs don't become unmanageable for students, many of whom are already struggling financially."[5]

College affordability remains "one of the biggest challenges facing higher education, now and into the future, as evidenced by increasing student loan debt,"[6] said Linda Oubré, the former president of Whittier College, an HSI located in California, about twenty miles from Los Angeles. According to the Department of Education, about six million students received Pell Grant funding in the 2020–21 academic year, yet the total student loan debt reached $1.75 trillion by the end of 2022. "On top of that, we have huge demographic shifts—fewer high school graduates, the traditional college-going market, with increasing proportions of students of color, Latinx in particular. Yet to keep our economy going, we need more graduates of higher education institutes."[7]

To keep up with this economic disparity, more colleges and universities shifted their financial aid approach. By 2016, more colleges and universities were using their institutional aid to woo wealthy students who could pay instead of using it to help low-income students to make up the difference between what their federal Pell Grants covered and what it costs to go to college. Those key findings were revealed in a groundbreaking report titled *Undermining Pell: The News Keeps Getting Worse for Low-Income Students.* The report—authored by Stephen Burd of the New America Foundation—found that "hundreds of colleges expect the neediest to pay an amount that equals more than half of their families' yearly earnings."[8] The report noted that too many four-year-colleges—both public and private—have failed to help the government achieve national college access goals. "They are, instead, adding hurdles that could stymie the educational progress of needy students or leave these students with mountains of debt after they graduate," the report noted.[9]

At the time of its release, the report drew mixed reactions among those who specialized in higher education policy. The report found that "many private colleges that have the means to enroll a substantial share of Pell Grant recipients and charge them a low price choose not to do so."[10] These included some of the country's most exclusive colleges, which tend to have generous financial aid policies but few low-income students, the report noted. "They also include a large number of colleges that use their institutional aid as a competitive weapon to attract the students they desire, rather than to meet the financial need of their students."[11]

The report also found that

- 775 private colleges, or 94 percent of those examined, charged first-year students with family incomes of $30,000 or less an average net price of over $10,000;

- 596, or 72 percent, charged over $15,000;

- 246, or 30 percent, charged over $20,000; and

♦ 85, or 10 percent, required these students to come up with an average of more than $25,000 each year.

The report indicated that the proportion of Pell Grant recipients that colleges enrolled and the net price those students were charged "is closely tied to the schools' wealth."[12] For instance, at 590 private colleges—or 72 percent of those examined—Pell Grant recipients made up 25 percent or more of the student body. "The median endowment for these schools was $31 million, and the median net price they charged the lowest-income freshmen was $17,189," the report noted.[13] In contrast, the report noted that at 62 private colleges, or 8 percent of those examined, Pell Grant recipients made up less than 15 percent of the institutions' student bodies. "The median endowment for these schools was $662 million, and the median net price they charged the neediest freshmen was $11,894," the report concluded. "This is not, however, just a question of wealth," Burd wrote. "There were 102 private colleges with endowments of more than $250 million that charged low-income freshmen an average net price over $10,000; 72 that charged over $15,000; 41 that charged over $20,000; and 20 that charged over $25,000."[14]

On a more detailed level, of those schools,

♦ 364, or 44 percent, had their average net price increase by at least $1,000;

♦ 227, or 28 percent, had their average net price increase by at least $2,500; and

♦ 75, or 9 percent, had their average net price increase by at least $5,000.

And during that same period, the report found that

- ♦ the number of private colleges that charged the most financially needy students an average net price over $15,000 grew to 594—or 72 percent of those examined—from 563, or 69 percent, and

- ♦ the number of private colleges that charged the lowest-income students an average net price over $20,000 rose to 245—or 30 percent of those examined—from 224, or 27 percent.

But a handful of colleges were in fact bucking the trend.

To wit, there were 25 private nonprofit colleges where Pell Grant recipients made up more than 15 percent of students but charged the lowest-income students average net prices of less than $10,000. "Twelve of these colleges are among the wealthiest higher education institutions in the country," the report stated. "Of the 12 wealthy colleges on the list, three have Pell enrollments over 20 percent or more." Those three schools—Amherst College, Columbia University, and Grinnell College— "generally have strong leaders who have made a personal commitment to making their campuses, which have long been among the most elite in the country, socioeconomically diverse,"[15] the report stated. "In so doing, they have bucked conventional wisdom and have shown that even the most selective schools can find large numbers of low-income students who can thrive at their institutions," it continued.[16] Nearly half of the 591 public four-year colleges and universities examined enroll at least 25 percent low-income students and charge the neediest first-years a net price of less than $10,000, Burd's report noted. "But don't be fooled," Burd wrote.

"Over the past two decades, there has been a fundamental shift in the admissions practices of many public universities."[17]

THE SECOND CHANCE PELL EXPERIMENT

As a national debate raged on in Washington, DC, in 1994 about how best to meet the expanding number of inmates locked up in America's prisons, Senator Pell made the decision to publicly weigh in and offered a forceful plea. Pell tried, without much success, to argue that the Pell Grant—named after him—should be extended to those behind bars. Education, he said, "is our primary hope for rehabilitating prisoners. Without education, I am afraid most inmates leave prison only to return to a life of crime."[18] Congress, however, ignored his appeal and instead passed legislation that restricted inmates from accessing the grant. The decision was part of the litany of "tough on crime" policies that permeated much of the 1990s. It would take a twenty-six-year fight to restore Pell Grants for those incarcerated, but that process would be long and arduous. Advocates hailed the move as an opportunity for 760,000 people in prison to achieve a better life through education.

In July 2022, Miami Dade College (MDC) in Florida became one of the first colleges and universities to award associate degrees to incarcerated students after the Pell funding was restored. At Everglades Correctional Institution, eighteen inmates were awarded their degree. The students made up MDC's first class as part of the Second Chance Pell Experiment, a 2015 initiative of the Obama administration that was created to make federal Pell Grants available to prisoners once again. While serving their sentences, the students took full course loads, including classes in philosophy, chemistry, and Spanish, allowing them to complete their degrees in a year and a half. The path was not easy for students or administrators—the program kicked off in January 2021, amid the COVID-19 pandemic.[19]

Although the Second Chance Pell Experiment was controversial when it was first announced, with Republicans arguing that President Obama had overstepped his authority, the program was expanded by both the Trump and Biden administrations and has been supported by celebrities and social influencers, including Kim Kardashian. Even before the grants became more widely available, MDC had plans to expand its offerings. Sixteen of the graduates who were still incarcerated back in 2022 began taking classes toward a bachelor's degree, and a new cohort of associate degree students had already enrolled. MDC opened a similar program at the Everglades Re-Entry Center, a different prison on the same grounds.

More than 40 million Americans have benefited from the Pell Grants. These first-generation college students, veterans, adult learners, and those incarcerated represent a varied cross section of society. Educational advocates are now asking a series of critical questions about how the Pell Grant program can evolve to better support students in nontraditional educational pathways, including online learning and competency-based education. With student loan debt reaching crisis levels, how can the principles behind Pell Grants inform broader reforms in higher education financing? While Pell Grants have dramatically increased access to higher education, challenges remain in ensuring that recipients complete their degrees. How can the program be refined to support not just access but also success? In an era of increasing political polarization, how can Pell's legacy of bipartisan cooperation in support of education be maintained and strengthened? As other nations invest heavily in higher education, how can programs like Pell Grants ensure that the US remains competitive in the global knowledge economy?

7 | ADAM CLAYTON POWELL AND THE BLACK CHURCH

As I walk the streets of the Harlem's of the world, the Black Harlem's and the white Harlem's, people are depressed. They are frustrated. They're downtrodden. They see no hope. They see no tomorrows. And I say to them always—keep the faith, baby. I say this because all of the world, people are not receiving God. They're not getting the assurances that once were given. Promises have been broken and their dawn refuses to rise. They're walking in the midnight of sorrow, in the midnight of frustration, in the midnight of despair. Too long have they been promised the good life by the great white fathers. Too long have they waited in vain, black and white, poor and illiterate, for the better jobs, better housing, better education, better hospitals—yet the conditions have not changed except for those who have always lived in the penthouses. For the people who live in the basements, in the cellar, their lives are still drab, ugly, have no hope, and I say to them keep the faith, baby.

> Congressman Adam Clayton Powell,
> in a speech titled "Keep the Faith,
> Baby," delivered in 1967

In the 1950s and 1960s, the fight for racial justice and civil rights in the United States was greatly aided by the powerful leadership of Adam Clayton Powell Jr., the boisterous but well-respected politician who hailed from the belly of New York's most famous Black neighborhood: Harlem.

BEGINNING IN HARLEM

A towering figure in American political history, Powell's life and career were deeply intertwined with the struggle for civil rights and educational equity. Powell was born on November 29, 1908, in New Haven, Connecticut, to a family of prominent religious leaders. His father, Adam Clayton Powell Sr., was a well-known Baptist minister and Powell would go on to follow in his father's footsteps to lead one of Harlem's most treasured religious institutions: Abyssinian Baptist Church. At the same time, he would emerge as one of the most influential African American politicians of the twentieth century.

There's no question that Powell's formative years played a major role in shaping his worldview and ambitions. From his early schooling to his time at Colgate University and Columbia University, these educational experiences not only equipped Powell with the knowledge and skills he would later employ in his political career but also instilled in him a deep appreciation for the transformative power of education and his desire to help make college more affordable and accessible to all Americans, regardless of their race or economic background. Powell's record in this arena is clear. He helped to increase federal support for college students and institutions.

His remarkable life sat at the intersection of education, civil rights, and political power in mid-twentieth-century America. His father was born into slavery in Franklin County, Virginia, in 1865 and his mother, Mattie Shaffer Fletcher Powell, came from a mixed-race background. Her influence on Adam Jr.'s early life was significant, instilling in him a strong sense of racial pride and a commitment to social justice that would characterize his political career many years later.

In 1908, the same year Adam Jr. was born, his father relocated the Abyssinian Baptist Church from West Fortieth between Seventh and Eighth Avenues in the red-light district of midtown Manhattan to Harlem. This move coincided with the beginning of the Great Migration, a period that saw millions of African Americans relocate from the rural South to urban areas in the North. Suddenly, Harlem had quickly become the cultural capital of Black America—the Mecca—and the birthplace of the Black literary and music movements. And the Powell family was right at the center of this transformation.

Growing up in Harlem during this pivotal time had a profound impact on young Adam. Not only was he exposed to the vibrant cultural and intellectual life of the Harlem Renaissance, surrounded by artists, writers, and thinkers who were redefining African American identity and challenging racial stereotypes, but he also developed an early commitment to civil rights.

Initially, he enrolled at City College in New York but later transferred to Colgate University upstate. After he graduated from Colgate in 1930, Powell earned a master's degree in religious education from Columbia University. It was at Colgate and Columbia where his ideas about the need for higher education started to blossom. When Powell entered Colgate in 1926, there were only four other African American men in the entire student body: Merton Anderson, Ray Vaughan, Daniel Crosby, and John Enoch. All the men except Powell participated in Colgate athletics and hailed from modest backgrounds. According to Powell's biographer, Wil Haygood, Powell—who was fair-skinned—initially tried to pass for white but later came to embrace his Blackness.[1] After Powell graduated from Colgate, he returned to the bustling Harlem community to become an assistant pastor at Abyssinian, the church that his father led from 1908 until his retirement in 1937. When Daddy Powell relinquished the pulpit to his son, the congregation at Abyssinian touted a membership list that stretched into the thousands and had emerged as one of the city's most prominent Black congregations. In addition to using the pulpit to work for social change and organize his community around issues related to discrimination in employment and government services, Powell successfully led the "Don't Buy Where You Can't Work" campaign, which succeeded in opening up jobs to African Americans at New York stores, utility companies, and city buses. One of his lieutenants, the Reverend Leon Sullivan, carried that campaign into Philadelphia, where it was not only successful but also became the precursor to Operation Breadbasket—the economic arm of the SCLC that was founded in 1957 by a host of civil rights titans that included Dr. Martin Luther King Jr., Ralph Abernathy, and others. Later, in 1967, King appointed a young country preacher from Greenville, South Carolina, to lead Breadbasket in Chicago. The young man's name was Reverend Jesse Louis Jackson Sr.

STEPPING INTO POLITICS

In 1941, Powell decided to run for a seat on the New York City Council, campaigning on a platform of civil rights and economic justice. His election made him the first African American to serve on the city council, marking a significant breakthrough in Black political representation in New York. As a city council member, Powell continued to advocate for the interests of his Harlem constituents while also addressing citywide issues. He pushed for increased funding for public housing, fought against discrimination in city hiring practices, and worked to improve public health services in underserved communities. Powell's success on the city council and his growing national profile as a civil rights leader set the stage for his next political move. In 1944, he decided to run for the US House of Representatives, seeking to represent New York's Twenty-Second Congressional District, which included Harlem. His campaign for Congress was marked by the same bold advocacy and charismatic leadership that had characterized his earlier work. Powell promised to be a fierce advocate for civil rights and economic justice in Washington, vowing to challenge the entrenched power structures that perpetuated racial inequality.

The congressional district had been redrawn in 1944, creating a Black-majority district for the first time. This redistricting reflected the changing demographics of New York City and the growing political power of the African American community.

During his campaign, Powell leveraged his reputation as a dynamic community leader and his extensive network in Harlem. His campaign platform focused on civil rights, economic justice, and increased opportunities for African Americans. He promised to be a vocal advocate for his constituents and to challenge the racial status quo in Washington. Powell's charismatic personality and his track record of activism made him a formidable candidate. He was able to mobilize a broad coalition of supporters, including church members, labor unions, and civil rights activists. His campaign was marked by energetic rallies and door-to-door canvassing, reflecting Powell's grassroots approach to politics. The election was held on November 7, 1944, and Powell won by a landslide, capturing over 75 percent of the vote. His victory was seen as a mandate from the people of Harlem and a sign of the changing political landscape in urban America.

Powell's election to Congress was significant for several reasons. He became only the fourth African American elected to Congress in the twentieth century and the first from New York State since Reconstruction. His election was part of a broader shift of African American voters toward the Democratic Party, a trend that would have lasting implications for American politics. Finally, his presence in Congress ensured that the concerns of urban African Americans would have a powerful advocate in the federal government. Upon his election, Powell made it clear that he intended to use his position to push for bold reforms. He famously declared, "My people need me in Washington," signaling his commitment to using his office as a platform for advancing civil rights and addressing the needs of his constituents.

Powell's election to Congress also marked a significant step in his personal journey. From the pulpit of the Abyssinian Baptist Church to the New York City Council, and now to the US House of Representatives, Powell had risen to a position of national influence. His educational background, which had equipped him with strong oratorical skills and a deep understanding of social issues, would prove invaluable in his new role.

As he prepared to take his seat in the Seventy-Ninth Congress, Powell was keenly aware of the challenges and opportunities that lay ahead. He would be entering a legislative body that was still overwhelmingly white and where many members were openly hostile to civil rights initiatives. However, Powell was determined to use his position to push for meaningful change. His election to Congress set the stage for a legislative career that would span more than two decades and leave a lasting impact on American civil rights legislation, including significant efforts to make higher education more accessible and affordable.

LEGISLATIVE PROGRESS

One of Powell's most significant contributions to education came through his role as chair of the House Education and Labor Committee, a position he held from 1961 to 1967. This powerful committee assignment allowed him to shape critical pieces of legislation that would have far-reaching impacts on American education. While not the primary sponsor, Powell played a crucial role in shaping and passing the National Defense Education Act of 1958 (NDEA). The act provided federal funding for education at all levels, with a particular focus on improving science, mathematics, and foreign language instruction. It also established the first federal student loan program, making higher education more accessible to millions of Americans.

Powell was deeply supportive of President Lyndon B. Johnson's HEA. This cornerstone of Johnson's Great Society program was shepherded through the House by Powell's committee. The act dramatically expanded federal funding for higher education, including establishing the BEOG (later renamed the Pell Grant), which provides need-based grants to low-income students; creating the Guaranteed Student Loan Program (later known as the FFEL Program); and providing funding for college libraries, student support services, and college work-study programs.

Powell supported the Elementary and Secondary Education Act of 1965, another key component of the Great Society. This act significantly increased federal funding for K–12 education and Powell was instrumental in its passage, ensuring that it included provisions to support schools serving low-income students and to promote school desegregation.

Powell supported expansions and improvements to the National School Lunch Act of 1946, which provided free or reduced-price lunches to school children from low-income families, recognizing the crucial link between nutrition and educational outcomes.

Powell backed the Library Services Act of 1956, which provided federal funding to establish and improve public libraries, particularly in rural areas. Powell was a proponent of community colleges as an affordable pathway to higher education and supported legislation to increase federal funding for community colleges and to improve transfer programs between two-year and four-year institutions.

Powell recognized that tuition was not the only financial barrier to college attendance. He advocated for programs to help students with other expenses, such as books, housing, and transportation. This included support for campus housing programs and expansion of college libraries. To ensure that federal education funds were being used effectively to benefit students, Powell used his position as chair of the Education and Labor Committee to conduct oversight hearings. He investigated instances of misuse of funds and pushed for greater accountability in how colleges and universities used federal assistance. He fought against discriminatory practices in higher education that effectively made college more expensive for minority students. This included challenging institutions that received federal funds but maintained segregationist policies.

Because Powell's platform extended beyond the sacred halls of Congress, he had the captive audience of a politically active Black church, which had been a driving force for Black mobility since Africans arrived on these shores. Powell's fervent devotion to the improvement of education and his tireless attempts to democratize access to postsecondary education by means of financial aid programs would have a lingering impact on a generation of other Black legislators like Congressman William H. Gray III, who like Powell, was not only a politician; he was also the influential pastor of the historic Bright Hope Baptist Church in Philadelphia. Powell's impressive track record would greatly influence Gray, who after rising through the ranks of Congress to become House Minority Whip from 1989 to 1991, would go on to helm one of the most powerful higher education advocacy organizations for African Americans in the country: the UNCF. Powell's advocacy on the higher education front also deeply inspired and influenced Congressman Floyd Flake, the former pastor of the Greater Allen A. M. E Church, who would represent Queens, New York, in Congress from 1987 to 1997. Flake later served as president of his alma mater, Wilberforce University, an HBCU located in Ohio.

Powell's rise in Congress came as the burgeoning civil rights movement was in full swing. His competitive adversary—Dr. Martin Luther King Jr.—had already successfully staged a boycott in Montgomery, Alabama, to call attention to the segregation of the Jim Crow South, as Thurgood Marshall and other leaders from the NAACP Legal Defense Fund worked tirelessly to desegregate schools in the landmark *Brown v. Board of Education* case.

But what about higher education, which was mostly a prerogative of the wealthy? As a result of discriminatory admissions rules, large pockets of Black Americans were denied access to the advantages of a college degree. From his perch in Congress, Powell saw this discrepancy as an obvious barrier to social advancement and set out to fight and alter the status quo. He fought tenaciously to establish financial aid programs for impoverished students and supported key legislation designed to increase federal financing for HBCUs. His impact on the NDEA, for instance, was one of his most notable accomplishments. He saw the act as a chance to address wider educational gaps even though it was originally intended to increase education in science and technology in reaction to the Soviet Union's launch of Sputnik.

While Powell embraced federal student loan programs, acknowledging that they had in fact helped millions of people pursue higher education throughout the years, he was also keenly aware that the student loan system had rightfully drawn criticism for leaving graduates with a hefty debt burden even in those early years. His focus and strategy, instead, was to link the pursuit of an education to civil rights and health care. His belief was that if all Americans—particularly Black Americans—had access to an education, basic civil rights, and health care, they could in fact prosper in society and care for their families.

And he would call upon his congregation at Abyssinian to help.

IMPACT OF THE BLACK CHURCH

The one powerful institution in the country that has consistently understood economic empowerment has been the Black Church. It is no coincidence then, that it would be Powell—the preacher turned politician—who would be among those who would help to usher in legislation that would champion access to higher education for all, not a select few.

Whether in Compton or Cleveland, or Atlanta or Atlantic City, the United States has had a long history of Black churches and other religious organizations giving money to youngsters seeking a college education. Such financial support has been particularly instrumental in the lives of African Americans, whose denominations and local congregations have helped fund postsecondary education for high school graduates since Blacks first gained access to college campuses. Churches have raised funds in a variety of ways, from fish fries, cake walks, and ice cream socials to budget line items, a special category offering envelopes and impromptu "love" offerings to students who need last-minute help with books, transportation, or incidentals. Whether the aid is $250 or $2,500, Black churches large and small, urban and rural, have continually helped to ease what can be a major financial burden for students. Their backing represents the continuation of the history of the Black Church as an institution that has endeavored to meet the growing needs of

Black people in every aspect of life and an institution that fundamentally views education as key to upward mobility.

Since the establishment of HBCUs, denominations such
as Baptist and African Methodist Episcopal—which founded
a number of the HBCUs—have provided institutional support
while many local congregations give directly to their youngsters,
said Eddie S. Glaude Jr., a professor at Princeton University
and graduate of Morehouse College, the nation's only HBCU
created for African American men. "For Black churches, education has been a paramount goal," he said. "Local churches
have supported education as a primary vehicle to aspiration for
the next generation. It's been important particularly for rural
communities where kids went off and went away to college."[2]

At Black churches like Harlem's Abyssinian Baptist Church,
scholarship funds are as common as food pantries, with awards
often disbursed in the spring at a formal presentation in front
of the congregation and usually for the first year of school.
Sometimes the amount is a few hundred dollars, enough to
cover some books, meals, or transportation. Other times, the
amounts are more substantial, often depending on factors such
as a church's membership size and the number of students
who receive money. "The more we invest in our students, the
greater the dividends,"[3] said Rev. Nelson B. Rivers II, pastor of
Charity Missionary Baptist Church located in Charleston, North
Carolina. Rivers graduated from Wilberforce University more
than five decades ago and served for twenty years on its board
of trustees. Each year, Rivers and his church send several of his
young congregants to his alma mater. Other students have gone
on to Hampton University and Howard University. His church,
which has about eight hundred members, created a program

called Diamond Minds, a scholarship initiative that provides up to $1,000 to student recipients. The money "goes for books, but sometimes it's getting them there," he said.[4] For twins Shaun and Sherita Ingram of Ohio, the $400 scholarships from their home church, Hosack Street Baptist Church in Columbus, helped them to pay for various school-related expenses during their time in college. The recent college graduates received family-sponsored scholarships and federal aid to help offset their loans. Sherita, who graduated from Reynoldsburg High School's health science and human services academy, earned a nursing degree from Bowling Green State University and has aspirations of becoming a nurse anesthetist. During her time at Bowling Green, she was active in SMART, a campus peer-mentoring program for students of color that promotes academic achievement. Shaun, who graduated from their high school's STEM academy, got involved in Young Life and Cru student faith organizations at Miami University of Ohio. He also joined the rowing team. He studied biophysics with a premed emphasis and has plans to someday become a doctor.

At the multicampus St. Stephen Baptist Church based in Louisville, Kentucky, those students who graduate from high school and plan to start college the same year must be interviewed as part of an application process, said the program's director, Rev. Pat Taylor. Since the program's inception in 2012, St. Stephen has awarded more than one hundred students financial assistance ranging from $500 to $3,500. While some programs are selective, awarding money to only its top applicants, many churches try to provide some amount to every applicant.

Several years ago, Virginia Union University, an HBCU in Richmond, teamed up with the Baptist General Convention of

Virginia to encourage churches to sponsor students. If a church provided a $3,000 scholarship to a student, the university would match it. The effort was aimed at eliminating student debt and preventing students who enroll in college from dropping out because their funds dried up. Technically, scholarships should be paid to the student's college—or reported by the student if they receive it directly—so that financial aid advisers can adjust the student's financial aid plan, said Jill Desjean, a senior policy analyst with the National Association of Student Financial Aid Administrators. Black churches, however, sometimes issue the payment to the student personally, sometimes out of ignorance and other times thinking the student and family can best determine how it should be used—or to prevent the school from cutting back on other aid the student will receive. "Eligibility for financial aid is limited by the cost of attendance,"[5] said Desjean. "Outside money, regardless of where it comes from, is considered 'estimated financial aid' and has to be factored into a student's financial aid package." Such aid, Desjean said, can be applied to decrease a student's loans or work-study employment or to reduce scholarship aid a student is to receive from the institution, called "scholarship displacement."

Rivers said that members of his congregation–many of whom were not able to earn a college degree themselves—have long been committed to helping younger churchgoers with their college education. "I'm glad that the church has agreed and is willing and excited,"[6] said Rivers, who had contemplated a career in the United States Air Force until someone encouraged him to consider college. "I remember well how many people looked out for me, many who I didn't know. We have to do that for others."

8 | PILLARS OF SUPPORT
TMCF, UNCF, and NAFEO

As a proud graduate of Howard University, I know first-hand that our HBCUs are centers of academic excellence. For generations, these anchors of our communities have played a pivotal role in building and contributing to America's leadership at home and abroad. Today, graduates from our Nation's more than 100 HBCUs are in every room where important decisions are made—leading in our schools, hospitals, courtrooms, boardrooms, and at the highest levels of government. And as we look forward, we know that our HBCUs will continue to prepare young leaders to build a better, more just future for our country and the world.

Vice President Kamala Harris, in a White House
statement made in May 2024

The Thurgood Marshall College Fund (TMCF), the United Negro College Fund (UNCF), and the National Association for Equal Opportunity in Higher Education (NAFEO) have not only been instrumental in shaping the narrative of higher education for minority students but have also played a pivotal role in making college more affordable and accessible for countless individuals. These advocacy organizations have collectively worked to bridge the gap in providing educational opportunities and financial resources for students attending HBCUs and PBIs. From providing scholarships and internships to advocating for policy changes and institutional support, these organizations have created a multifaceted approach to addressing the complex issue of college affordability.

THE UNITED NEGRO COLLEGE FUND

For millions of Americans, Lou Rawls—the velvet-voiced singer known for his smooth baritone and genre-spanning career—became the public face of the UNCF for more than two decades. Rawls singlehandedly supported the philanthropic and advocacy organization that provided scholarships to students attending private HBCUs across the nation. From 1980 until his death in 2006, Rawls hosted the *Lou Rawls Parade of Stars* telethon and called on his celebrity friends to help him annually raise more than $200 million for UNCF. When Anheuser-Busch signed the crooner to become their national spokesperson, they asked Rawls which charity he wanted the brewing company to support as part of his contract. Though he was not a college graduate himself, Rawls immediately pointed to UNCF and branded the telethon so that it carried his name. The fundraiser featured comedy and musical performances from various artists in support of the UNCF's efforts. The televised event became a who's who of entertainment and included prominent artists like Ray Charles, Stevie Wonder, and Michael Jackson.

Born in Chicago in 1933, Rawls overcame a challenging childhood to become one of the most versatile and respected vocalists of his generation. His career spanned gospel, jazz, soul, and pop, showcasing his remarkable range and distinctive voice. But it was UNCF's mission of promoting higher education opportunities for African American students and strengthening HBCUs that captured Rawls's interests. "He's just someone who recognized, like many African Americans of a certain generation, that education was something that our kids didn't get access to and that it was critically important for their future, and for our communities' future and for the nation," said Dr. Michael Lomax, president and CEO of the UNCF.[1]

Rawls's efforts went beyond just fundraising. He became a passionate advocate for education, often speaking about its importance in empowering individuals and communities. His famous catchphrase, "A mind is a terrible thing to waste," became synonymous with the UNCF's mission. For years, UNCF had relied on African American entertainers from the Motown era to generate millions of dollars for the organization's coffers. But after Rawls died from cancer, there was a growing sense that the organization had to cultivate new support from young Black Hollywood if it was expected to raise funds. Lomax enlisted support from celebrities such as Jussie Smollett, Anthony Anderson, Kevin Hart, Usher, and Ludacris.

The UNCF was founded in 1944. During World War II and the ongoing struggle for civil rights, Dr. Frederick D. Patterson, president of what is now Tuskegee University, recognized the need for a united front to support the nation's HBCUs and their students. Along with educator and activist Mary McLeod Bethune and other HBCU leaders, Patterson established UNCF as a fundraising organization to pool the resources of HBCUs and create a centralized scholarship fund for African American students. The timing of UNCF's founding was crucial. It came at a period when racial segregation was still legally enforced in much of the United States and educational opportunities for African Americans were severely limited. HBCUs played a vital role in providing higher education to Black students, and UNCF emerged as a critical support system for these institutions and their students. UNCF set out to build a robust and nationally recognized pipeline of underrepresented students who, because of UNCF support, would become highly qualified college graduates. As the largest and most effective minority education organization in the United States, UNCF has expanded its role beyond merely providing scholarships to become a comprehensive support system for both students and member institutions.

UNCF's approach to making college more affordable is multifaceted and addresses various aspects of the higher education journey. At the heart of UNCF's work are its extensive scholarship programs. These range from general scholarships open to all eligible students to specialized awards for specific fields of study, regions, or demographic groups. UNCF administers over four hundred scholarship programs. UNCF also provides crucial financial support to its thirty-seven member institutions. This support helps these HBCUs keep their tuition rates lower, indirectly benefiting students by making education at these institutions more affordable. Recognizing that unexpected financial hardships can derail a student's education, UNCF operates an emergency student aid program. This initiative provides just-in-time financial support to students at risk of dropping out due to unpaid tuition balances, textbook costs, or other education-related expenses. UNCF operates several programs aimed at preparing students for college success, including the

UNCF Empower Me Tour and the UNCF Portfolio Project. By improving college readiness, these programs help students maximize their chances of completing their degrees efficiently, thus reducing the overall cost of their education.

UNCF engages in policy advocacy and conducts research to promote policies that make college more affordable for minority students. This includes advocating for increased federal student aid, support for HBCUs, and policies that address systemic barriers to higher education. Its Career Pathways Initiative was funded by a $50 million grant from the Lilly Endowment. This initiative helps students at UNCF member institutions prepare for careers in the twenty-first-century workplace. The impact of UNCF's work over its nearly eighty-year history has been profound. Since its founding, UNCF has raised more than $5 billion to support its member institutions and has helped more than five hundred thousand students earn college degrees. UNCF reports that the six-year graduation rate for UNCF scholarship recipients is 70 percent, significantly higher than the national average for all students and nearly twice the rate for all African American students.[2] A 2017 study by UNCF found that UNCF member institutions and their alumni generate $14.8 billion in annual economic impact and over 134,000 jobs.[3] Even more impressive is that UNCF member institutions, which represent only 3 percent of all four-year colleges, produce almost 20 percent of all African American college graduates.[4] UNCF member HBCUs are responsible for 25 percent of all STEM degrees awarded to African American students, playing a crucial role in diversifying these critical fields.[5]

UNCF has continually innovated to meet the changing needs of students and the evolving higher education landscape.

In 2014, the nonprofit launched the UNCF/Koch Scholars Program with a $25 million grant from Koch Industries and the Charles Koch Foundation. The program provides scholarships, mentorships, and entrepreneurial education to high-achieving African American students. A year later, UNCF created its Career Pathways Initiative. This program helps UNCF member institutions strengthen career placement outcomes for their graduates through curriculum enhancements, faculty development, and employer partnerships. This work is enhanced by the UNCF National Alumni Council, which supports current students through mentorship, networking, and philanthropic giving. Finally, the UNCF Institute for Capacity Building provides technical assistance to UNCF member institutions to enhance their operational and academic capabilities.

Given the importance of STEM fields in the modern economy, UNCF is increasing its focus on supporting students pursuing STEM degrees. The organization is also leveraging technology to enhance its scholarship application process, mentoring programs, and support services and has intensified its efforts to help member institutions enhance their financial stability, academic offerings, and operational efficiency. UNCF continues to advocate for policies that address systemic barriers to higher education for minority students, including increased federal support for HBCUs and reforms to student financial aid programs. UNCF's enduring commitment to making college affordable and accessible for African American students has left an indelible mark on American higher education. Through its comprehensive approach, innovative programs, and unwavering advocacy, UNCF continues to play a crucial role in opening doors of opportunity and fostering the next generation of African American leaders.

THE THURGOOD MARSHALL COLLEGE FUND

The TMCF was established in 1987 by Dr. N. Joyce Payne. The organization bears the name of the first African American Supreme Court justice, Thurgood Marshall, who was appointed to the high court in 1967 by President Lyndon B. Johnson. This choice of namesake is no coincidence; it reflects the organization's commitment to justice, equality, and the transformative power of education—values that Justice Marshall championed throughout his illustrious career. TMCF was founded with a specific focus on supporting students attending public HBCUs and PBIs. The organization's mission is multifaceted: to ensure student success, promote academic excellence, and prepare the next generation of leaders emerging from HBCUs. TMCF's approach to making college more affordable is comprehensive and goes beyond simply providing financial assistance. The organization has developed a holistic strategy that addresses various aspects of the college experience. At the core of TMCF's efforts are its scholarship and grant programs. These financial aid packages are designed to alleviate the burden of tuition and other college-related expenses. TMCF offers a variety of scholarships, including merit-based awards, need-based grants, and scholarships focused on specific fields of study. TMCF recognizes that affordable education isn't just about student finances—it's also about institutional strength. The organization works directly with HBCUs to enhance their capacity to serve students effectively. This includes providing resources for faculty development, improving campus infra-structure, and supporting academic program enhancements. TMCF understands that the value of a college education extends beyond the classroom. The organization has developed robust career development programs, including internships, mentorship opportunities, and job placement services. Connecting students with career opportunities, TMCF helps ensure that the investment in college education translates into tangible career outcomes. Through various initiatives, TMCF cultivates leadership skills among HBCU students. These programs not only enhance students' college experiences but also prepare them for future success, increasing the long-term value of their education. TMCF engages in advocacy efforts at both state and federal levels to promote policies that support HBCUs and their students. This work includes lobbying for increased federal funding for HBCUs and pushing for policies that address systemic barriers to higher education for minority students. The impact of TMCF's work is best illustrated through the success stories of its scholars and member institutions. Since its inception, TMCF has awarded over $300 million in assistance to its students and member institutions. This financial support has made college a reality for thousands of students who might otherwise have found higher education out of reach. TMCF scholars consistently demonstrate high academic achievement. The organization reports that its scholars maintain an average GPA of 3.5 or higher, showcasing how financial support coupled with academic resources can drive excellence. Through its career development programs, TMCF has helped place thousands of students in internships and full-time positions with Fortune 500 companies and government agencies. This success in job placement demonstrates how TMCF's approach extends beyond college affordability to long-term career success. TMCF's support has helped member institutions enhance their academic offerings, improve retention rates, and increase graduation rates. For example, several TMCF member institutions have seen significant increases in their six-year graduation rates following partnerships with TMCF.

TMCF's advocacy efforts have contributed to several policy victories, including increased federal funding for HBCUs and the preservation of key financial aid programs that benefit minority students. The Thurgood Marshall College Fund stands as a testament to the power of targeted, comprehensive support in making college more affordable and accessible. Through its multifaceted approach, TMCF continues to open doors of opportunity for countless students, strengthen HBCUs, and contribute to a more equitable higher education.

THE NATIONAL ASSOCIATION FOR EQUAL OPPORTUNITY IN HIGHER EDUCATION

Unlike TMCF and UNCF, which focus primarily on providing direct financial support to students and institutions, the NAFEO was established in 1969, a pivotal year in the civil rights movement and a time of significant change in American higher education. NAFEO emerged as a response to the unique challenges faced by HBCUs and PBIs in the wake of desegregation and the ongoing struggle for equal educational opportunities. NAFEO's mission centers on advocacy, research, and capacity building. NAFEO was founded by HBCU presidents and chancellors who recognized the need for a unified voice to advocate for the interests of HBCUs and PBIs at the federal level. The organization's creation came at a time when many HBCUs were facing financial difficulties and questions about their relevance in a post-segregation era. NAFEO's founders understood that these institutions continued to play a vital role in providing higher education opportunities for African American students and needed strong advocacy to ensure their survival and growth.

NAFEO serves as the "voice for Blacks in higher education," representing the interests of over one hundred HBCUs and PBIs at the federal and state levels. NAFEO's key objectives include championing the interests and programs of HBCUs and PBIs; providing services to NAFEO members; serving as a clearinghouse for information and as an instrument of technical assistance for HBCUs and PBIs; and interpreting and articulating the need for and characteristics of HBCUs and PBIs. While NAFEO doesn't directly provide scholarships, its work is crucial in making college more affordable for students at HBCUs and PBIs by advocating for policies and funding that support these institutions and their students.

NAFEO employs several strategies to enhance college affordability for students at HBCUs and PBIs and works tirelessly to secure federal funding for HBCUs and PBIs. This includes advocating for increased appropriations in the federal budget, support for HBCU-specific programs, and expanded student financial aid. NAFEO conducts research on issues affecting HBCUs and PBIs, including college affordability. This research informs policy recommendations aimed at making higher education more accessible and affordable for minority students. Through various initiatives, NAFEO helps HBCUs and PBIs enhance their operational efficiency and effectiveness. This includes providing technical assistance, sharing best practices, and facilitating partnerships. By strengthening these institutions, NAFEO indirectly contributes to making education more affordable and accessible for students. NAFEO facilitates partnerships between HBCUs/PBIs and private sector companies. These partnerships often result in internship opportunities, scholarship programs, and other initiatives that help make college more affordable for students. In addition to its federal advocacy work, NAFEO engages with state governments to secure funding and support for public HBCUs. This work is crucial in ensuring that state-funded HBCUs receive equitable resources, which in turn helps keep tuition costs manageable for students. NAFEO promotes financial literacy programs at member institutions, helping students make informed decisions about financing their education and managing their resources effectively.

While NAFEO's impact on college affordability is often indirect, it has been substantial. Through its advocacy efforts, NAFEO has helped secure significant increases in federal funding for HBCUs and PBIs. For example, NAFEO played a key role in advocating for the FUTURE Act, signed into law in 2019, which permanently reauthorized $255 million in annual mandatory funding for HBCUs and other MSIs. NAFEO's policy work has contributed to changes that benefit HBCU students. This includes improvements to the PLUS loan program, which many HBCU students rely on to finance their education. By helping HBCUs and PBIs improve their operations and secure resources, NAFEO has contributed to the financial stability of these institutions. This stability allows these schools to keep tuition costs lower and offer more institutional aid to students. NAFEO's advocacy has helped raise the profile of HBCUs and PBIs, leading to increased philanthropic support and corporate partnerships.

Looking to the future, NAFEO is focusing on several key areas, including intensifying its efforts to support STEM education at HBCUs and PBIs, recognizing the growing importance of these fields. The organization is working to facilitate more international partnerships for HBCUs and PBIs, expanding opportunities for students and institutions. NAFEO is investing in data analytics to strengthen its advocacy efforts and demonstrate the impact of HBCUs and PBIs more effectively. NAFEO is increasing its focus on aligning HBCU and PBI programs with workforce needs, enhancing the value proposition of education at these institutions. NAFEO's unique role in advocating for HBCUs and PBIs has been crucial in shaping policies and securing resources that make college more affordable for countless students. While its impact may be less direct than scholarship-granting organizations, NAFEO's work in strengthening the overall ecosystem of HBCUs and PBIs is fundamental to the long-term affordability and accessibility of higher education for minority students.

JOINT ADVOCACY EFFORTS

While TMCF, UNCF, and NAFEO have distinct missions and approaches, their work often intersects and complements each other in ways that amplify their individual impacts on college affordability. One of the most significant areas of collaboration among these organizations is in their advocacy efforts. TMCF, UNCF, and NAFEO often join forces to lobby for policies and funding that benefit HBCUs, PBIs, and their students. The three organizations, along with other HBCU-focused groups, form a powerful coalition that speaks with a unified voice on issues affecting HBCUs and their students. This coalition has been instrumental in securing bipartisan support for HBCU funding and programs.

TMCF, UNCF, and NAFEO collaborate with the White House Initiative on HBCUs to organize the annual HBCU

Week Conference. This event brings together HBCU leaders, federal agencies, and private sector partners to discuss challenges and opportunities in HBCU education, including issues of affordability. The organizations often participate jointly in this conference, using it as a platform to advocate for HBCU interests and discuss strategies for enhancing college affordability for minority students. TMCF, UNCF, and NAFEO frequently collaborate on research projects and share data to strengthen their collective understanding of the challenges facing HBCUs and their students. This shared knowledge base informs their individual and joint strategies for addressing college affordability. UNCF and NAFEO have collaborated on studies examining the economic impact of HBCUs, providing crucial data to support advocacy efforts for increased funding. The organizations share research on factors influencing student success at HBCUs, including financial challenges and effective support strategies.

While each organization has its unique programs, there are areas where their efforts complement each other. NAFEO, which doesn't directly provide scholarships, often refers students to scholarship opportunities offered by TMCF and UNCF. TMCF and UNCF's internship and career development programs often benefit from NAFEO's policy work and institutional capacity-building efforts. NAFEO's work in strengthening HBCU operations complements the institutional support provided by TMCF and UNCF, creating a more comprehensive support system for these schools.

The COVID-19 pandemic had a profound impact on higher education, particularly on HBCUs and their students. TMCF established an emergency fund to provide direct financial assistance to students facing hardships due to the pandemic. The organization quickly pivoted to virtual formats for its leadership development programs and career fairs, ensuring continued support for students despite campus closures. Recognizing the psychological toll of the pandemic, TMCF expanded its mental health resources for scholars, addressing a critical need that impacts student success and retention.

During the pandemic, UNCF launched a campaign to raise funds specifically for emergency student aid, helping students cover unexpected expenses related to campus closures and remote learning. UNCF advocated for increased funding to address the digital divide exposed by the shift to online learning, pushing for resources to ensure HBCU students had access to necessary technology. The organization also provided guidance and resources to help its member institutions navigate the challenges of remote instruction and campus safety protocols.

On the legislative front, NAFEO played a crucial role in advocating for the inclusion of HBCUs in the CARES Act and subsequent relief packages, securing critical funding for these institutions and their students. The organization facilitated knowledge sharing among its member institutions on best practices for remote learning and student support during the pandemic. NAFEO has been working with policymakers to address the long-term financial implications of the pandemic on HBCUs and their students, advocating for sustained support beyond the immediate crisis.

Recent years have seen growing recognition of the vital role HBCUs play in higher education, potentially leading to increased support and resources. Many companies are expanding their diversity and inclusion efforts, creating new opportunities for partnerships with organizations supporting HBCU students.

While disruptive, new technologies also offer opportunities to enhance educational delivery, improve operational efficiency, and expand reach. There's potential for increased international collaborations, offering new opportunities for HBCU students and institutions. The TMCF, UNCF, and NAFEO have each played crucial roles in making college more affordable and accessible for students at HBCUs and PBIs. Through their diverse approaches—from direct financial aid to policy advocacy and institutional support—these organizations have collectively shaped the landscape of higher education for minority students in the United States. Their work has not only impacted individual students but has also strengthened HBCUs and PBIs, ensuring these vital institutions continue to serve as engines of opportunity and mobility. As they face future challenges, from technological disruption to demographic shifts, these organizations will need to continue adapting and innovating. However, their core missions remain as relevant and crucial as ever. In a society still grappling with racial and economic inequalities, the work of TMCF, UNCF, and NAFEO in championing college affordability for minority students is not just about education—it's also about building a more equitable and prosperous future for all Americans.

As we look ahead, it's clear that these organizations will continue to play pivotal roles in shaping the future of higher education. Their success will be measured not just in dollars raised or policies changed but also in the countless lives transformed through the power of affordable, accessible higher education. The challenges are significant but so, too, are the opportunities to create lasting, positive change in American society through the empowerment of the next generation of leaders from HBCUs and PBIs.

9 | THE COLLEGE FOR ALL ACT

Today, we say to our young people that we want you to get the best education that you can, regardless of the income of your family. Good jobs require a good education. That is why we are going to make public colleges and universities tuition free and cancel all student debt.

Vermont Senator Bernie Sanders, in a presidential campaign speech delivered in 2019

Bernie Sanders—the self-described socialist senator from Vermont and former presidential candidate, put forward a plan in 2021 to make college free for all Americans. "In the wealthiest country in the history of the world, a higher education should be a right for all, not a privilege for the few,"[1] Sanders said, announcing the legislation that received support in the House of Representatives from Congresswoman Pramila Jayapal, a Democrat from Washington.

The College for All Act could have been the answer to the decades-old student debt crisis. The legislation, which sought to amend the HEA, pushed for the elimination of tuition and fees at public four-year colleges and universities for those making up to $125,000. Community college tuition and fees would be waived.

The College for All Act was introduced by Sanders (I-VT) in the Senate in 2017, with an updated version reintroduced in 2021, whereas Representative Pramila Jayapal (D-WA) introduced a companion bill in the House of Representatives. The act emerged from a growing concern over the rising costs of higher education and the burden of student debt on millions of Americans. The College for All Act proposed several sweeping changes to the current higher education system, namely free tuition at public institutions. The act proposed to eliminate tuition and fees at public four-year colleges and universities for families earning up to $125,000 per year—about 80 percent of the population—and make community college free for all. The legislation would have provided at least $41 billion per year to states and tribes to eliminate undergraduate tuition and fees at public colleges and universities and institutions of higher education controlled by tribes. All students—regardless of income—would also be able to attend community colleges tuition- and fee-free.

If enacted, the federal government would have covered 67 percent of the costs of eliminating tuition and fees at public colleges and universities and tribal institutions of higher education. States and tribes would have been responsible for eliminating the remaining 33 percent of the costs. To qualify for federal funding, states and tribes would need to meet several requirements designed to protect students, ensure quality, and reduce ballooning costs. States and tribes would also need to maintain spending on their higher education systems, on academic instruction, and on need-based financial aid. In addition, colleges and universities would commit to reducing their reliance on low-paid adjunct faculty. No funding under this legislation could be used to fund administrator salaries, merit-based financial aid, or the construction of nonacademic buildings like stadiums and student centers. "If we are going to have the kind of standard of living that the American people deserve, we need to have the best educated workforce in the world,"[2] Sanders said.

THE FREE COLLEGE MOVEMENT

The free college movement gained some traction during the 2016 presidential campaign, when Sanders made free public college a central plank of his platform. Since then, the idea has become a mainstream policy proposal within the Democratic Party, with various candidates and elected officials proposing different versions of free college plans. The free college movement represents the latest chapter in a long history of efforts to expand access to higher education in the United States. It builds upon the legacy of land-grant colleges, the GI Bill, and federal student aid programs while also responding to the unique challenges of the twenty-first century. As we delve deeper into the movement's arguments, proposals, and potential impacts, it is crucial to keep this historical context in mind. The debate over free college is not just about education policy; it is also fundamentally about what kind of society we want to build and how we value knowledge and opportunity in the modern world.

One of the primary arguments for free college is that it would significantly expand access to higher education, particularly for low-income and underrepresented students. Proponents argue that the current system, with its high tuition costs and complex financial aid process, creates significant barriers for many potential students. By eliminating tuition, free college would remove a major obstacle that prevents many students from pursuing higher education. This could lead to increased enrollment rates, particularly among first-generation college students and those from low-income backgrounds. The current system of financial aid, with its myriad of grants, loans, and scholarships, can be overwhelming and confusing. A free college system would simplify this process, making it easier for students and families to understand their options and plan for higher education. Given that students of color and those from low-income families are disproportionately burdened by student debt, free college could help address long-standing inequities in higher education access and outcomes.

Another key argument for free college is that it represents a crucial investment in the nation's human capital and long-term economic competitiveness. In an increasingly knowledge-based economy, a more educated workforce is essential for economic growth and innovation. Free college could help ensure that the US has the skilled workers needed to compete in the global economy. By making higher education more accessible, free college could enhance social mobility, allowing more individuals to move up the economic ladder and contribute to overall economic growth. In a rapidly changing job market, the ability to retrain and acquire new skills throughout one's career is increasingly important. Free college could make it easier for adults to return to school and adapt to changing economic conditions.

Many advocates of free college argue that it would represent a return to the idea of higher education as a public good rather than a private commodity. Proponents often point to the success of previous initiatives like the GI Bill and the historically low tuition at many public universities as evidence that free or low-cost higher education is both possible and beneficial.

Higher education provides benefits that extend beyond the individual student, including a more informed citizenry, increased civic engagement, and broader cultural enrichment. Free college would recognize and enhance these public benefits. By removing price tags from public higher education, free college could help shift the focus away from viewing education primarily as a private investment and toward seeing it as a public good that benefits society as a whole.

Free college is often proposed as a policy tool to combat growing income inequality in the United States. By making higher education more accessible, free college could help break intergenerational cycles of poverty, allowing more individuals to access high-paying jobs and career opportunities. Student debt has been shown to exacerbate wealth gaps, particularly along racial lines. Free college could help address these disparities by eliminating a major source of debt for many families. Proponents argue that free college represents a progressive economic policy that would disproportionately benefit lower- and middle-income families, helping to reduce overall economic inequality.

While the free college movement has gained significant traction and support, it also faces numerous challenges and criticisms. Understanding these counterarguments is crucial for a comprehensive analysis of the issue. One of the primary criticisms of free college programs is their potential cost to taxpayers and questions about how they would be funded.

CRITICS OF TUITION-FREE COLLEGE

Critics argue that making public colleges tuition-free would place an enormous burden on state and federal budgets. The cost could potentially lead to tax increases or cuts in other important areas of public spending. There are concerns about the long-term sustainability of free college programs, especially during economic downturns when government revenues decrease but demand for education often increases. Some argue that the money required for free college could be better spent on other educational initiatives, such as improving K–12 education or expanding targeted aid to the neediest students. While proponents argue that free college would promote equity, critics raise several counterpoints. Some argue that universal free college could be regressive, as it would provide a subsidy to middle- and upper-income families who can afford to pay for college, potentially at the expense of other programs that benefit lower-income individuals. There are concerns that free public college could negatively impact private colleges and universities, potentially reducing educational diversity and choice. Critics question the fairness of implementing free college for future students while those who have already incurred student debt would not benefit. Some argue that making college free could have unintended consequences on the quality of education and access to it. If free tuition leads to increased enrollment without corresponding increases in funding and capacity, it could result in overcrowding at public institutions, potentially reducing the quality of education. There are concerns that free tuition could strain institutional resources, leading to larger class sizes, fewer course offerings, or reduced student services. Some worry that institutions might face pressure to lower standards or inflate grades to justify continued funding in a free college system. Critics raise concerns about how free college might impact the labor market and individual career choices: if a college degree becomes the new baseline expectation for employment, it could lead to credential inflation, potentially devaluing bachelor's degrees and pushing students toward costly graduate education. There are concerns that free college could encourage more students to pursue fields that may not align with job market demands, potentially exacerbating underemployment among college graduates. Some argue that removing the price signal from higher education could reduce incentives for students to complete their degrees efficiently or make cost-effective educational choices.

The practical challenges of implementing a free college program are often cited by critics. There are debates about whether free college should be a federal- or state-level initiative, with concerns about maintaining local control and accommodating regional differences. Questions arise about what exactly would be covered under a free college program. Would it include just tuition or also fees, books, and living expenses? How would part-time students be treated? There are concerns that free college programs could lead to increased government control over higher education institutions, potentially compromising their autonomy and academic freedom.

Several states have implemented their own versions of free college programs, often called Promise programs. These initiatives offer valuable case studies for understanding the potential impacts and challenges of free college on a larger scale.

TENNESSEE PROMISE

Launched in 2014, the Tennessee Promise program offers tuition-free community college or technical school to all high school graduates in the state. Key features include last-dollar scholarships, which cover tuition and fees not met by other grants and scholarships. There is also a mentoring program to support students through the college application and transition process, a community service requirement, and a minimum GPA requirement to maintain eligibility. Early results have shown increased enrollment in community colleges and technical schools, though there have been challenges in retention and completion rates.

Brianna Lopez found a beacon of hope in an envelope that arrived just weeks before her high school graduation. Inside was the confirmation of her Tennessee Promise scholarship, a ticket to a future she had long dreamed of but wasn't sure how to achieve.

"When I got that letter, it felt like the whole world opened up," Lopez recalled. "Suddenly, college wasn't just a dream anymore. It was a real possibility."[3] The Tennessee Promise scholarship program, launched in 2015, offers last-dollar scholarships to high school graduates, covering tuition and mandatory fees not met by the Pell Grant, the HOPE Scholarship, or other state student assistance funds. For students like Lopez, whose parents hadn't attended college and who faced financial constraints, the program represented a lifeline to higher education. "My parents always encouraged me to go to college, but we didn't know how we'd afford it," Lopez said. "Tennessee Promise changed everything for us."

The scholarship allowed Lopez to enroll at Southwest Tennessee Community College without the burden of tuition costs. But the program offered more than just financial support. It also provided a structured path to success that began even before Lopez set foot on campus. "There were mandatory meetings we had to attend during our senior year of high school," she remembered. "At first, I thought they might be boring, but they turned out to be incredibly helpful. We learned about the college application process, financial aid, and what to expect in college. It made the whole thing a lot less intimidating."

Another crucial component of the Tennessee Promise program is mentorship. Each scholar is paired with a mentor who guides them through the college preparation process and their first semester of college. "My mentor was amazing," said Lopez. "She helped me stay on track with all the scholarship requirements and was always there to answer my questions. Having someone who believed in me and understood the system made a huge difference."

The scholarship came with certain requirements that Lopez had to meet to maintain her eligibility. These included maintaining a 2.0 GPA, completing eight hours of community service each term enrolled, and attending mandatory meetings. "The requirements kept me focused," she said. "Knowing I had to maintain my grades and do community service pushed me to manage my time better and stay committed to my studies."

The community service aspect, in particular, had a profound impact on Lopez. "I volunteered at a local animal shelter," she said. "It not only fulfilled the scholarship requirement but also helped me discover a passion for animal welfare that I might not have otherwise found."

As Lopez progressed through her program at Southwest Tennessee Community College, she found that the benefits of Tennessee Promise extended beyond just covering tuition. "Because I didn't have to worry about how to pay for classes, I could focus more on my studies and really engage with my education," she said. "I was able to join study groups, participate in campus activities, and even take on a part-time job to cover my other expenses without feeling overwhelmed."

The program's design, which encourages students to complete their associate's degree in two years, also helped Lopez stay on track. "The structure of the program motivated me to take a full course load each semester," she said. "It was challenging at times but knowing that I had this amazing opportunity pushed me to make the most of it." Two years after receiving that life-changing letter, Lopez stood proudly at her college graduation, with an associate's degree in hand. But her educational journey didn't end there. "Tennessee Promise gave me such a strong foundation," she said. "After completing my associate's degree, I felt prepared and motivated to continue my education."

Lopez went on to transfer to the University of Memphis to pursue a bachelor's degree, a step she's not sure she would have taken without her experience in the Tennessee Promise program. "The program didn't just give me a degree," Lopez added. "It gave me confidence in my abilities and a clear vision for my future. It showed me what I was capable of achieving."

As Lopez works on completing her bachelor's degree, she remains grateful for the opportunity Tennessee Promise provided. "I'm the first in my family to go to college," she said, her voice filled with pride. "Tennessee Promise made that possible. It's not just a scholarship program—it's a promise of a better future, and for me, that promise was fulfilled."

NEW YORK'S EXCELSIOR SCHOLARSHIP

Introduced in 2017, the Excelsior Scholarship aims to make public colleges tuition-free for middle-class New York residents. Notable aspects include an income cap, initially set at $100,000 and later increased to $125,000. Recipients are required to live and work in New York for a period after graduation. The program also includes credit requirements to ensure timely degree completion. While the program has expanded access, critics have noted that its structure may exclude many low-income students and part-time learners.

OREGON PROMISE

Established in 2015, Oregon Promise provides grants to cover tuition at Oregon community colleges. Those who partici- pate must have a minimum high school GPA requirement. The program has shown success in increasing community college enrollment, particularly among first-generation college students.

COLLEGE FOR ALL

Sanders's act sought to expand the Promise programs to a federal initiative. Doing so, he argued, would cut student loan interest rates and allow existing borrowers to refinance their loans at lower rates. The act would also triple federal investment in work-study programs and increase support for HBCUs and other MSIs. The proposed funding would have come primarily from a tax on Wall Street financial transactions, including stock trades, bonds, and derivatives.

Put simply, the College for All Act was rooted in several key theoretical principles—namely, that education should be viewed as a public good. This view posits that a more educated populace benefits society through increased innovation, civic engagement, and economic productivity. By making college more accessible, the act aims to promote economic mobility and reduce inequality. The theory is that removing financial barriers to higher education will allow more individuals from lower-income backgrounds to obtain degrees, potentially leading to higher-paying jobs and breaking cycles of poverty. Proponents argued that reducing or eliminating student debt would act as a significant economic stimulus. The theory suggests that freed from heavy debt burdens, graduates would have more disposable income to invest, save, or spend, thereby boosting economic activity. The act was partly motivated by a desire to keep the United States competitive in the global economy. By increasing the number of college graduates, the country aims to maintain a highly skilled workforce capable of driving innovation and economic growth.

The proposal faced significant political hurdles, including that the plan was too expensive to implement and questions about the feasibility of funding it through the proposed Wall Street tax. Some argued that the plan is too broad and that free college should be more targeted to those in financial need. There were concerns about how the act might affect private colleges and universities, which are not directly covered by the legislation. While supporters argue the act would stimulate the economy, critics worry about potential negative effects on the financial sector due to the proposed tax. Some policymakers prefer alternative approaches to making college more affordable, such as expanding existing financial aid programs or focusing on reducing the cost of higher education.

Still, the College for All Act represented a bold vision for transforming higher education in the United States. While its future remains uncertain, the proposal has sparked a national and important conversation about the future of access to higher education for millions of Americans who wonder if a college education is within their reach.

10 | SOLUTIONS FOR THE FUTURE

The roots of the student debt crisis are multifaceted, stemming from rising tuition costs, stagnant wages, and a job market that increasingly demands higher education credentials. While much attention has been focused on government policies and potential federal solutions, this chapter explores how the private sector is addressing the student debt crisis.

In recent years, a diverse array of private sector actors has stepped up to tackle the student debt crisis. These efforts range from corporate benefit programs to innovative financial technology solutions, each approaching the problem from a different angle. The private sector's involvement brings fresh perspectives, technological innovation, and significant financial resources to bear on this complex issue. Over the years, *Diverse* has written extensively about many of these efforts and the ways that they are working to alleviate the crisis.

CORPORATIONS

On the corporate front, many companies have recognized that student debt is not just a personal problem for their employees but also a factor that affects workplace productivity, employee retention, and overall economic health. In response, a growing number of corporations have launched initiatives to help employees manage and repay their student loans. One of the most direct ways companies are addressing the student debt crisis is through student loan repayment assistance programs. These programs typically involve the employer making direct payments toward an employee's student loan debt, often as part of the overall benefits package.

For example, PwC (PricewaterhouseCoopers) was one of the early adopters of this approach. Their program offers associates and senior associates up to $1,200 per year toward student loan debt for up to six years. This benefit can potentially reduce student loan principal and interest obligations by as much as $10,000 and shorten loan payoff periods by up to three years. Similarly, Fidelity Investments offers employees a student loan repayment program that contributes up to $15,000 toward employees' student loans. The program has proven popular, with over twelve thousand employees taking advantage of it within its first five years. Another approach some companies are taking is to offer education benefits that can help employees avoid taking on additional debt while advancing their careers. Amazon's Career Choice program is a prime example of this strategy.

Amazon's program prepays 95 percent of tuition and fees for employees to earn certificates and associate degrees in high-demand occupations such as aircraft mechanics, computer-aided design, machine tool technologies, medical lab technologies, and nursing. By focusing on in-demand fields, this program not only helps employees avoid additional student debt but also improves their long-term career prospects. These corporate initiatives represent a significant shift in how companies view their role in addressing societal issues like student debt. They recognize that by helping to alleviate this burden, they can improve employee satisfaction, retention, and productivity while also contributing to broader economic stability.

NONPROFITS

While for-profit companies have significant resources to bring to bear on the student debt crisis, nonprofit organizations play a crucial role in advocacy, education, and direct support to borrowers. These organizations often focus on systemic change and support for the most vulnerable borrowers.

The Student Debt Crisis Center (SDCC) is a nonprofit organization dedicated to fundamentally reforming the way we pay for higher education in the United States. SDCC takes a multipronged approach to addressing the student debt crisis. SDCC lobbies for policy changes at both the state and federal levels, pushing for reforms such as increased funding for public higher education and expansion of loan forgiveness programs. The organization provides resources and information to help borrowers understand their rights and options for managing their student debt. SDCC also offers direct support to borrowers through their Student Debt Relief Helpline, which provides free guidance on loan repayment options, forgiveness programs, and loan servicers.

Young Invincibles is a national nonprofit focused on amplifying the voices of young adults in the political process. While their work covers a range of issues affecting millennials and Gen Z, student debt is a key focus area. The organization conducts and publishes research on the impact of student debt on young adults, informing policy discussions and public discourse. It advocates for policies to make higher education more affordable and to provide relief to current borrowers. Young Invincibles runs financial literacy programs to help young adults make informed decisions about education financing and debt management.

The Institute for College Access & Success (TICAS) is a nonprofit organization working to make higher education more available and affordable for people of all backgrounds. Their work on student debt includes policy research and recommendations. TICAS produces in-depth research on student debt and college affordability, using this to inform policy recommendations. The organization's Project on Student Debt provides annual updates on student debt levels and other key metrics, which are widely cited in discussions of the crisis. TICAS advocates for reforms to the student loan system, including simplification of income-driven repayment plans and increased state funding for public higher education.

These nonprofit organizations play a vital role in the ecosystem of private sector efforts to address the student debt crisis. They often work in tandem with corporate initiatives and government programs, providing crucial research, advocacy, and direct support to borrowers.

AFTERWORD

Keeping Hope Alive: The Long Arc of the Student Debt Movement in an Era of Political Resistance

The 2024 election of Donald J. Trump alongside a Republican Congress marks a sad and devastating moment in the ongoing struggle for student debt relief in America. There is no question that the political landscape has shifted dramatically, requiring a fundamental reassessment of strategies and priorities for those committed to addressing the student debt crisis.

The immediate implications of this political realignment are stark. The US Department of Education, under Republican leadership, signals a return to policies that could severely impact borrower protections. Congressional leadership has already outlined plans to dismantle key programs, including potential restrictions on income-driven repayment plans and the elimination of Public Service Loan Forgiveness. These changes threaten to unravel years of incremental progress in making higher education more accessible and debt management more feasible for millions of Americans. And Trump—even before he took office in January 2025—campaigned on a promise that he would ultimately dismantle the Department of Education.

As I noted throughout this book, the student debt crisis remains one of the most pressing civil rights issues of our time, with implications that cut across racial, economic, and generational lines. Black borrowers carry a disproportionate burden, holding nearly 50 percent more debt on average than their white counterparts four years after graduation. Women hold roughly two-thirds of all student debt, creating a gender-based disparity that compounds existing wage gaps. These statistics reflect systemic inequities that the new administration's policies threaten to exacerbate.

The Republican Congress has signaled its intent to pursue several troubling policy changes. First, any proposals to cap or eliminate Grad PLUS loans would devastate graduate education accessibility, particularly affecting HBCUs and other MSIs, where these loans are crucial for professional advancement. Second, plans to privatize aspects of federal loan servicing could remove crucial consumer protections and oversight mechanisms, potentially leading to predatory practices similar to those seen in the subprime mortgage crisis. Finally, proposed changes to Pell Grant funding formulas could reduce access for the most economically vulnerable students, forcing them to take on even more debt or abandon their educational aspirations entirely.

The election of Trump and a conservative-leaning Congress also presents opportunities for strategic innovation at the federal level. The movement for student debt relief must evolve beyond traditional advocacy approaches and develop a multilayered response to these new political realities.

State-level action will become increasingly crucial in this new environment. Several states have already implemented promising programs that could serve as national models. For instance, Massachusetts's Student Loan Bill of Rights provides robust borrower protections that could be replicated elsewhere. Maine's student loan tax credit program offers relief through the state tax code, demonstrating how states can provide tangible benefits even when federal policy is hostile. The regulatory framework at the state level offers another avenue for progress. State attorneys general have significant authority to oversee loan servicers and protect borrowers from predatory practices. This authority becomes even more critical as federal oversight will undoubtedly weaken under the Trump administration.

Looking ahead to the 2026 midterms and beyond, several strategic priorities must emerge. First, the student debt movement must focus on building durable political power that can withstand administrative changes. This requires developing sophisticated voter education and mobilization programs specifically focused on student debt issues. The demographic shifts in the electorate— with millennials and Gen Z comprising an increasingly large share of voters—create potential for building a powerful voting bloc around educational equity issues. Second, advocates must develop protection strategies for existing programs while simultaneously advancing new solutions. This includes strengthening state-level oversight of loan servicers; developing alternative financing mechanisms through state governments; creating public-private partnerships for debt relief; establishing strong legal frameworks to protect borrower rights; and building strong coalitions with labor union, civil rights organizations, and professional associations. Third, the movement needs to reframe the narrative around student debt in ways that resonate across ideological lines. Emphasizing economic growth, workforce development, and American competitiveness can help build broader support for debt relief policies, even in red states.

More importantly, the role of higher education institutions must evolve in response to this new political reality. Universities and colleges need to develop institutional loan relief programs, implement cost containment measures, create emergency aid programs, and reform financial aid packaging to minimize student borrowing and strengthen partnerships with state governments and private sector entities. My institution—Trinity Washington University—has already started to move in this direction.

There's no question that the Trump administration's approach to higher education financing represents more than just a policy shift—it signals a fundamental challenge to the very idea of education as a public good. The student debt relief movement must respond not only with tactical adjustments but also with a renewed articulation of why accessible, affordable higher education matters for America's future. The legal framework for protecting borrower rights will become increasingly important under this administration. Strategic litigation, state-level consumer protection laws, and regulatory oversight mechanisms will play crucial roles in maintaining basic protections for student borrowers. The movement must invest in legal infrastructure while simultaneously building political power for longer-term change.

The fundamental challenge facing the student debt movement in this era is not just political but moral: how to maintain momentum for systematic change while protecting vulnerable borrowers from immediate harm. The answer lies in building stronger coalitions, developing more sophisticated policy tools, and maintaining focus on both immediate protection and long-term transformation.

With the next presidential election around the corner, the movement for student debt relief and educational equity faces its greatest test yet. The current political environment demands not just resistance but reimagination—of strategies, of coalitions, and of possibilities for change. The path forward will require unprecedented coordination between state governments, educational institutions, advocacy organizations, and affected communities.

The story of student debt relief in America continues to unfold. While the federal landscape presents significant challenges, the movement's strength lies in its adaptability, its growing sophistication, and its deep commitment to educational equity. The arc of history still bends toward justice—but in this era, we must be prepared to bend it ourselves, through sustained organizing, innovative policy solutions, and unwavering commitment to the principle that education is a right, not a privilege reserved for the wealthy.

ACKNOWLEDGMENTS

This book would not have been possible without the contributions of many individuals. I extend my deepest gratitude to the team at *Diverse: Issues In Higher Education*. For more than twenty years, I have had the privilege of being affiliated with the trade publication founded in 1984 by Dr. William E. Cox and Frank L. Matthews. Over the years, I have served the publication in numerous roles: senior staff writer, editor-at-large, managing editor, and executive editor.

For four decades, *Diverse* (which was founded as *Black Issues In Higher Education*) has been at the forefront of covering critical issues in higher education, and the insights gained from our collective work have been invaluable in shaping this book. I am profoundly grateful to the countless students, families, and educators who shared their personal stories and experiences with student debt over the years. Their voices form the heart of this work and drive home the urgency of addressing this pressing issue.

I offer my sincere thanks to the higher education researchers, policy experts, civil rights leaders, and financial aid administrators who generously offered their time and expertise to help me to understand this issue. Their data, analysis, and insights have been crucial in presenting a comprehensive picture of the student debt crisis. I would like to acknowledge the support of my colleagues in the education journalism community. Our ongoing dialogues and collaborations have enriched this book immeasurably.

To my editor and the publishing team at Broadleaf Books, particularly Lisa Kloskin, thank you for your guidance, patience, and belief in the importance of this project. Your commitment to excellence has elevated this work.

I am grateful to Patricia McGuire, president of Trinity Washington University. Trinity has served as my academic home and has supported my scholarly work as a professor and associate dean of graduate studies. President McGuire has provided me with the space and the time to pursue a host of intellectual endeavors and projects that align with my interests, and I am grateful to her and my provost, Dr. Carlota Ocampo, for their endorsement of my pursuits.

Finally, I owe an enormous debt of gratitude to my family and friends—particularly my parents and siblings—for their support and understanding throughout the writing process. Your encouragement has been my constant source of motivation. In October 2024, my dear mother passed away. I miss her guidance and her wisdom and will forever be thankful for all that she gave to me. A special shoutout to my loving wife, Jamila, and my son, Justin, who are my biggest cheerleaders.

This book is dedicated to all those striving for an education while grappling with the weight of student debt. May it contribute to a broader understanding of this issue and inspire meaningful change in our higher education system.

NOTES

INTRODUCTION

1. Shauntee Russell, personal interview with the author, June 10, 2024.
2. Aimee Picchi, "Two Courts Just Blocked Parts of Biden's SAVE Student Loan Repayment Plan. Here's What to Know," *CBS News*, June 25, 2024, https://www.cbsnews.com/news/student-loan-forgiveness-save-kansas-missouri-court-rulings-cbs-explains/.
3. Collin Binkley, "Biden Administration Canceling Student Loans for 160,000 Borrowers, Says It Will Erase $7.7 Billion in Debt," *PBS News*, May 22, 2024, https://www.pbs.org/newshour/politics/biden-administration-canceling-student-loans-for-160000-borrowers-says-it-will-erase-7-7-billion-in-debt.
4. Zack Friedman, "Student Loan Forgiveness: Young Republicans Support Student Loan Cancellation in Surprising New Poll," *Forbes*, May 19, 2022, https://www.forbes.com/sites/zackfriedman/2022/05/19/new-poll-young-voters-want-biden-to-cancel-student-loans-for-everyone/.
5. Hannah Hartig, "Democrats Overwhelmingly Favor Free College Tuition, While Republicans Are Divided by Age, Education," Pew Research Center, August 11, 2011, https://www.pewresearch.org/short-reads/2021/08/11/democrats-overwhelmingly-favor-free-college-tuition-while-republicans-are-divided-by-age-education/.
6. Aimee Picchi, "Biden Administration Cancels $7.7 Billion in Student Debt for 160,500 People. Here's Who Qualifies,"

CBS News, May 23, 2024, https://www.cbsnews.com/news/student-loan-forgiveness-7-7-billion-heres-who-qualifies-biden/.
7. "Civil Rights Principles for Student Loan Debt Cancellation," The Leadership Conference on Civil and Human Rights, April 18, 2021, https://civilrights.org/wp-content/uploads/2021/04/Civil-Rights-Principles-for-Student-Loan-Debt-Cancellation.pdf, 1.
8. "Civil Rights Principles," 1.
9. Elie Mystal, "The Student Debt Crisis? It's Infinitely Worse for Black Women," *The Nation*, April 12, 2022, https://www.thenation.com/article/politics/student-debt-black-women/.
10. Charles H. F. Davis III et al., *Legislation, Policy, and the Black Student Debt Crisis: A Status Report on College Access, Equity, and Funding a Higher Education for the Black Public Good*. National Association for the Advancement of Colored People, 2000. https://drive.google.com/file/d/1vr0w7yYIXIv5r60up-gQ7P2xv7sPZQ--/view.

CHAPTER 1: THE HIDDEN CRISIS

1. Brianna McGurran, "College Tuition Inflation: Compare the Cost of College over Time," *Forbes*, May 9, 2023, https://www.forbes.com/advisor/student-loans/college-tuition-inflation/#:~:text=In%201980%2C%20the%20price%20to%20attend%20a%20four-year,price%20increased%20to%20%2428%2C775.%20That%E2%80%99s%20a%20180%25%20increase.
2. "#DoublePell," National Association of Independent Colleges and Universities, n.d., https://www.naicu.edu/issues-advocacy/doublepell/making-the-case.
3. Pearl Stewart, "Survey Findings Spotlight Food, Housing Insecurity Among College Students," *Diverse Issues In Higher Education*, February 18, 2020, https://www.diverseeducation.com/latest-news/article/15106298/survey-findings-spotlight-food-housing-insecurity-among-college-students.
4. "Government Data Reveals 1 in 5 Undergrads Are Food Insecure," *Diverse Issues In Higher Education*, August 4, 2023, https://

www.diverseeducation.com/reports-data/article/15543689/
government-data-reveals-1-in-5-undergrads-are-food-insecure.
5. "Government Data Reveals."
6. "Government Data Reveals."
7. "Government Data Reveals."
8. "Government Data Reveals."
9. Jennifer Ma and Matea Pender, *Trends in College Pricing and Student Aid 2021* (College Board, 2021), https://research.collegeboard.org/media/pdf/trends-college-pricing-student-aid-2021.pdf.
10. Jamie Wood, personal interview with the author, January 7, 2023.
11. Cailyn Nagle, "A Survey of College Students and Textbook Affordability During the COVID-19 Pandemic," Student PIRGs, February 24, 2021, https://studentpirgs.org/2021/02/24/fixing-the-broken-textbook-market-third-edition/#:~:text=In%20 2020%2C%2065%20percent%20of%20students%20sur-veyed%20reported,one%20during%20the%20same%20 period%20the%20previous%20year.
12. Maria Sanchez, personal interview with the author, March 1, 2024.
13. Robert Carroll, personal interview with the author, March 18, 2024.
14. Joselin Williamson, personal interview with the author, March 22, 2024.
15. "*Some College, No Credential* Student Outcomes: 2024 Report for the Nation and States," National Student Clearinghouse Research Center, June 6, 2024, https://nscresearchcenter.org/some-college-no-credential/.
16. Rebecca Kelliher, "Stranded Credits from Students with Debt. Is a Bigger Shift Starting?" *Diverse Issues In Higher Education*, February 7, 2022, https://www.diverseeducation.com/students/article/15288165/cuny-suny-stopped-withholding-transcripts-from-students-with-debt-is-a-bigger-shift-starting.
17. Walter Hudson, "Trinity Washington University Settles More Than $1.8 Million in Balances for Nearly 400 Full-Time Undergraduates,"

Diverse Issues In Higher Education, July 21, 2021, https://www.diverseeducation.com/institutions/msis/article/15109695/trinity-washington-university-settles-more-than-18-million-in-balances-for-nearly-400-full-time-undergraduates.

18. Travis Loller, "Historically Black Colleges Work to Help Students Amid Virus," The Associated Press, May 15, 2020, https://www.localmemphis.com/article/news/education/historically-black-colleges-help-students-amid-coronavirus-covid-19/522-b81c5eba-5a71-4d8f-abaa-b88d98e41b23.
19. Jamal Watson, "Book Review: 'Pregnant Girl' Prompts Public Policy Discussion About Parenting Students," *Diverse Issues In Higher Education*, June 7, 2021, https://www.diverseeducation.com/latest-news/article/15109379/book-review-pregnant-girl-prompts-public-policy-discussion-about-parenting-students.

CHAPTER 2: A CIVIL RIGHTS ISSUE

1. Al Sharpton, personal interview with the author, August 25, 2023.
2. Sharpton, interview.
3. Sharpton, interview.
4. Sharpton, interview.
5. Robert F. Smith, "Speech to the Morehouse College Class of 2019," May 19, 2019, Morehouse College, transcript and audio, 35:55, https://robertfsmith.org/videos/robert-f-smiths-speech-at-the-135th-commencement-at-morehouse-college/.
6. "Morehouse Graduate 'Motivated to Go Change the World' After Billionaire Wipes Out Students' Loans," *CBC News*, May 20, 2019, https://www.cbsnews.com/news/morehouse-college-graduate-reacts-to-philanthropist-robert-smith-wiping-out-students-loans/.
7. Smith, "Speech."
8. Tylik McMillan, personal interview with the author, June 28, 2024.
9. McMillan, interview.
10. McMillan, interview.
11. Cheyanne M. Daniels, "NAACP, Other Groups Rally with Advocates for Student Debt Relief Ahead of Supreme Court

Decision," *The Hill,* June 20, 2023, https://thehill.com/homenews/education/4059235-naacp-rallies-for-student-debt-relief/.

12. Adam S. Minsky, "Biden Affirms: 'I Will Eliminate Your Student Debt,'" *Forbes,* October 7, 2020, https://www.forbes.com/sites/adamminsky/2020/10/07/biden-affirms-i-will-eliminate-your-student-debt/.

13. Daniels, "NAACP."

14. Daniels, "NAACP."

CHAPTER 3: REPARATIONS AND STUDENT DEBT

1. Glenn Thrush and Maggie Haberman, "Trump Gives White Supremacists an Unequivocal Boost," *New York Times,* August 15, 2017, https://www.nytimes.com/2017/08/15/us/politics/trump-charlottesville-white-nationalists.html.

2. Sheila Jackson Lee, "H.R. 40 Is Not a Symbolic Act. It's a Path to Restorative Justice," ACLU, May 22, 2020, https://www.aclu.org/news/racial-justice/h-r-40-is-not-a-symbolic-act-its-a-path-to-restorative-justice.

3. Kiana Cox and Khadijah Edwards, "3. Reparations for Slavery," Pew Research Center, August 30, 2022, https://www.pewresearch.org/2022/08/30/black-americans-views-on-reparations-for-slavery/.

4. Jamal Watson, "Higher Ed Institutions Wrestle with Reparations and Repentance," *Diverse Issues In Higher Education,* November 7, 2019, https://www.diverseeducation.com/home/article/15105755/higher-ed-institutions-wrestle-with-reparations-and-repentance.

5. Watson, "Higher Ed Institutions."

6. Movement for Black Lives, "Reparations," n.d., https://m4bl.org/policy-platforms/reparations/.

7. Ali Mir and Saadia Toor, "Racial Capitalism and Student Debt in the U.S.," *Organization* 30, no. 4 (2021), https://journals.sagepub.com/doi/10.1177/1350508421995762.

8. Andre M. Perry and Carl Romer, "Student Debt Cancellation Should Consider Wealth, Not Income," The Brookings Institution,

February 25, 2021, https://www.brookings.edu/articles/
student-debt-cancellation-should-consider-wealth-not-income/.
9. Perry and Romer, "Student Debt."

CHAPTER 4: FACTORS DRIVING THE
STUDENT DEBT CRISIS

1. Keith W. Olson, "The G.I. Bill and Higher Education, Success and Surprise," *American Quarterly* 25, no. 5 (December 1973), https://www.jstor.org/stable/2711698?origin=crossref.
2. Robert Nixon, personal interview with the author, April 23, 2023.
3. "Trends in College Pricing: Highlights," College Board, n.d., https://research.collegeboard.org/trends/college-pricing/highlights.
4. Andrew Gillen, *Introducing Bennett Hypothesis 2.0* (Center for College Affordability and Productivity, 2012), https://files.eric.ed.gov/fulltext/ED536151.pdf.
5. National Association of Student Financial Aid Administrators, *National Student Aid Profile: Overview of 2022 Federal Programs* (National Association of Student Financial Aid Administrators, 2022), https://www.nasfaa.org/uploads/documents/2022_National_Profile.pdf.
6. "Bankruptcy and Student Loans," EveryCRSReport.com, July 18, 2019, https://www.everycrsreport.com/reports/R45113.html.
7. Andrew Gillen, "Credential Inflation: What's Causing It and What Can We Do About It?" The James G. Martin Center for Academic Renewal, August 7, 2020, https://www.jamesgmartin.center/2020/08/credential-inflation-whats-causing-it-and-what-can-we-do-about-it/.
8. Elise Gould, "State of Working America Wages 2019," Economic Policy Institute, February 20, 2020, https://www.epi.org/publication/swa-wages-2019/.
9. Lawrence Mishel and Jori Kandra, "Wages for the Top 1% Skyrocketed 160% Since 1979 While the Share of Wages for the Bottom 90% Shrunk," *Working Economics Blog*, Economic Policy Institute,

December 1, 2020, https://www.epi.org/blog/wages-for-the-top-1-skyrocketed-160-since-1979-while-the-share-of-wages-for-the-bottom-90-shrunk-time-to-remake-wage-pattern-with-economic-policies-that-generate-robust-wage-growth-for-vast-majority/.

10. Jayson Albert, personal interview with the author, April 11, 2023.

11. US Department of Education, "Education Department Approves $5.8 Billion Group Discharge to Cancel All Remaining Loans for 560,000 Borrowers Who Attended Corinthian," press release, November 6, 2023, https://www.ed.gov/news/press-releases/education-department-approves-58-billion-group-discharge-cancel-all-remaining-loans-560000-borrowers-who-attended-corinthian-colleges.

12. Michael Mitchell, Michael Leachman, and Kathleen Masterson, "A Lost Decade in Higher Education Funding: State Cuts Have Driven Up Tuition and Reduced Quality," Center on Budget and Policy Priorities, August 23, 2017, https://www.cbpp.org/research/a-lost-decade-in-higher-education-funding.

13. Ylan Q. Mui, "Americans Saw Wealth Plummet 40 Percent from 2007 to 2010, Federal Reserve Says," *Washington Post,* June 11, 2012, https://www.washingtonpost.com/business/economy/fed-americans-wealth-dropped-40-percent/2012/06/11/gJQAllsCVV_story.html#.

14. Anthony P. Carnevale and Ban Cheah, *From Hard Times to Better Times: College Majors, Unemployment, and Earnings* (Georgetown University Center on Education and the Workforce, 2016), https://cew.georgetown.edu/wp-content/uploads/HardTimes2015-Report.pdf.

15. Owen Daugherty, "National Cohort Default Rate Drops Amid Pandemic Payment Pause," National Association of Student Financial Aid Administrators, September 30, 2021, https://www.nasfaa.org/news-item/26156/National_Cohort_Default_Rate_Drops_Amid_Pandemic_Payment_Pause.

16. Pete Benson. Personal interview with author, January 2024.

17. Andre M. Perry, Marshall Steinbaum, and Carl Romer, "Student Loans, the Racial Wealth Divide, and Why We Need Full Student Debt Cancellation," The Brookings Institution, June 23, 2021,

https://www.brookings.edu/articles/student-loans-the-racial-wealth-divide-and-why-we-need-full-student-debt-cancellation/.

18. Abigail Johnson Hess, "American Women Hold Two-Thirds of All Student Debt—Here's Why," *CNBC*, March 14, 2018, https://www.cnbc.com/2018/03/13/american-women-hold-two-thirds-of-all-student-debt-heres-why.html.
19. Megan Peterman, personal interview with the author, May 21, 2024.
20. Barbara Kehm, "How Germany Managed to Abolish University Tuition Fees," The Conversation, October 13, 2014, https://theconversation.com/how-germany-managed-to-abolish-university-tuition-fees-32529.
21. "National Information: Sweden," Eurydice, n.d., https://eurydice.eacea.ec.europa.eu/countries/sweden/national-student-fee#tab-1.
22. The Student Loans Company, *Student Loans in England: Financial Year 2018–19* (The Student Loans Company, 2019), https://assets.publishing.service.gov.uk/media/5d011c63e5274a3d2cb71a3c/slcsp012019.pdf.
23. Indira Duarte, "Top Six Advantages of Pursuing Higher Education in Canada Instead of the United States," Canadim, October 6, 2023, https://www.canadim.com/blog/6-reasons-why-students-choosing-study-in-canada-over-united-states/.
24. https://www.aph.gov.au/About_Parliament/Parliamentary_Departments/Parliamentary_Library/pubs/rp/rp1617/Quick_Guides/HELP.

CHAPTER 5: UNRAVELING THE HIGHER EDUCATION ACT OF 1965

1. Adam Liptak, "Supreme Court Rejects Biden's Student Loan Forgiveness Plan," *New York Times*, June 30, 2023, https://www.nytimes.com/2023/06/30/us/student-loan-forgiveness-supreme-court-biden.html.
2. "Supreme Court Rules Student Loan Forgiveness Unconstitutional," *Diverse Issues In Higher Education*, June 30, 2023, https://

www.diverseeducation.com/leadership-policy/article/15541620/
supreme-court-rules-student-loan-forgiveness-unconstitutional.

3. "Supreme Court Rules."
4. Adam Liptak, "Student Loan Forgiveness: Supreme Court Rules 6-3 Against Biden Plan," *New York Times*, June 30, 2023, https://www.nytimes.com/live/2023/06/30/us/student-loans-supreme-court-biden.
5. "Supreme Court Rules."
6. Katie Lobosco, "Biden's Student Loan Forgiveness Program Was Rejected by the Supreme Court. Here's What Borrowers Need to Know," *CNN*, June 30, 2023, https://www.cnn.com/2023/06/30/politics/biden-student-loan-forgiveness-supreme-court/index.html.
7. Caroline Vakil, "What 2024 Republicans Are Saying About the Supreme Court's Student Debt Ruling," *The Hill*, June 30, 2023, https://thehill.com/homenews/campaign/4076336-what-2024-republicans-are-saying-about-the-supreme-courts-student-debt-ruling/.
8. "Biden Announces New Plans for Student Debt Relief: Live Updates," *NPR*, June 30, 2023, https://www.npr.org/live-updates/supreme-court-student-loan-forgiveness.
9. Sameer Gadkaree, "TICAS Denounces Supreme Court Decision to Block One-Time Student Debt Relief Program," The Institute for College Access & Success, press release, June 30, 2023, https://ticas.org/affordability-2/ticas-denounces-supreme-court-decision-to-block-one-time-student-debt-relief-program/.
10. Student Borrower Protection Center, "Supreme Court Sides with Right-Wing Special Interests, Blocking President Biden's Student Debt Relief Plan," press release, June 30, 2023, https://protectborrowers.org/scotus-lawlessly-blocks-student-debt-relief/.
11. Michael Macagnone, "Supreme Court Strikes Down Biden Student Loan Cancellation Program," *Roll Call*, June 30, 2023, https://rollcall.com/2023/06/30/supreme-court-strikes-down-biden-student-loan-cancellation-program/.

12. Devin Dwyer and Alexandria Hutzler, "Supreme Court Strikes Down Student Loan Forgiveness Program, Biden Pushing Ahead with New Plan," ABC News, June 30, 2023, https://abc7.com/student-loan-forgiveness-update-biden-debt-supreme-court-case-federal-relief/13231489/.

13. "Supreme Court Rules."

14. Lauren Egan, "'I Will Not Make That Happen': Biden Declines Democrats' Call to Cancel $50K in Student Debt," *NBC News*, February 17, 2021, https://www.nbcnews.com/politics/joe-biden/i-will-not-make-happen-biden-declines-democrats-call-cancel-n1258069.

15. Michael D. Shear, Jim Tankersley, and Zolan Kanno-Youngs, "Biden Gave In to Pressure on Student Debt Relief After Months of Doubt," *New York Times*, August 26, 2022, https://www.nytimes.com/2022/08/26/us/politics/biden-student-loans.html.

16. Robin Givhan, "Words That Matter: 'White Supremacy Is a Poison,'" *Washington Post*, May 17, 2022, https://www.washingtonpost.com/nation/2022/05/17/words-that-matter-white-supremacy-is-poison/o.

17. Minsky, "Biden Affirms."

18. Minsky, "Biden Affirms."

19. Julia Conley, "AOC Says Biden's Student Debt Relief Plan Could be Better," *Salon*, May 28, 2022, https://www.salon.com/2022/05/28/aoc-says-bidens-student-debt-relief-plan-could-be-better_partner/#:~:text=Rep.%20Alexandria%20Ocasio-Cortez%20on%20Friday%20joined%20economic%20justice,it%20most%20while%20excluding%20many%20desperate%20for%20relief.

20. Jamaal Abdul-Alim, "Higher Education Analysts Sound Caution on Obama Student Loan Relief Plan," *Diverse Issues In Higher Education*, October 26, 2011, https://www.diverseeducation.com/students/article/15090961/higher-education-analysts-sound-caution-on-obama-student-loan-relief-plan.

21. Orlando Mayorquin, "Where Did Biden Go to College? Biden Mentions Own Education During Loan Forgiveness Speech,"

USA Today, August 24, 2022, https://www.usatoday.com/story/news/politics/2022/08/24/where-did-joe-biden-go-college/7888214001/.

22. Mayorquin, "Where Did Biden Go to College?"

23. "Biden Details $10K Student Loan Debt Forgiveness for Borrowers Making Under $125K a Year," Yahoo!News, August 24, 2022, https://www.yahoo.com/news/biden-details-10k-student-loan-194606754.html.

24. Phil Mattingly, Katie Lobosco, and Maegan Vazquez, "Biden Announces Student Loan Relief for Borrowers Making Less Than $125,000," *CNN*, August 24, 2022, https://edition.cnn.com/2022/08/24/politics/student-loans-joe-biden-white-house/index.html.

25. "Taxpayers Association Challenges Governor's Abuse of Partial Veto Power," Brown County Taxpayers Association, n.d., https://www.bctaxpayers.com/press/.

26. "Roll Out of Student Debt Relief Portal Receives High Marks," *Diverse Issues In Higher Education*, October 18, 2022, https://www.diverseeducation.com/leadership-policy/article/15301810/roll-out-of-student-debt-relief-portal-receives-high-marks.

27. "Roll Out of Student Debt Relief."

28. "Roll Out of Student Debt Relief."

29. "Roll Out of Student Debt Relief."

30. "Roll Out of Student Debt Relief."

31. "Roll Out of Student Debt Relief."

32. "Student Borrowers Speak Out at Hearing on New Debt Relief Plan," *Diverse Issues In Higher Education*, July 18, 2023, https://www.diverseeducation.com/leadership-policy/article/15542597/student-borrowers-speak-out-at-hearing-on-new-debt-relief-plan.

33. Maxwell Alejandro Frost (@MaxwellFrostFL), "Just applied to an apartment in DC where I told the guy that my credit was really bad. He said I'd be fine. Got denied, lost the apartment, and the application fee. This ain't meant for people who don't already have money," Twitter (now X), December 8, 2022, https://x.com/MaxwellFrostFL/status/1600890367586406400?lang=en.

34. Maria Carrasco, "Biden's Debt Relief Plan Heads to Negotiated Rulemaking Public Hearing," National Association of Student Financial Aid Administrators, July 19, 2023, https://www.nasfaa. org/news-item/31209/Biden_s_Debt_Relief_Plan_Heads_to_ Negotiated_Rulemaking_Public_Hearing.
35. Phillip Oliff, "At What Cost? The Impact of Student Loan Default on Borrowers," The Pew Charitable Trusts, February 16, 2023, https://www.pewtrusts.org/en/research-and-analysis/ issue-briefs/2023/02/at-what-cost-the-impact-of-student-loan-default-on-borrowers.
36. Lyndon B. Johnson, "Remarks After a Meeting with Representatives of the American Bankers," June 10, 1966, https://www. presidency.ucsb.edu/documents/remarks-after-meeting-with-representatives-the-american-bankers-association-connection.

CHAPTER 6: THE ARCHITECT OF THE PELL GRANT

1. Wayne G. Miller, *An Uncommon Man: The Life and Times of Senator Claiborne Pell* (University Press of New England, 2011).
2. Associated Press, "Claiborne Pell Dies at 90; Former Rhode Island Senator, Creator of Pell Grants," *LA Times,* January 2, 2009, https:// www.latimes.com/local/obituaries/la-me-pell2-2009jan02-story.html.
3. "Quotation #32160," The Quotations Page, accessed January 31, 2025, http://www.quotationspage.com/quote/32160.html.
4. "Federal Pell Grant Program of the Higher Education Act: Primer," Congressional Research Service, updated November 6, 2024, https://crsreports.congress.gov/product/pdf/r/r45418, 38.
5. Liann Herder, "Pell Grant Increase Will Help Low-Income Students, But More Is Needed," *Diverse Issues In Higher Education,* January 4, 2023, https://www.diverseeducation.com/students/article/15305083/ pell-grant-increase-will-help-lowincome-students-but-more-is-needed.
6. Herder, "Pell Grant Increase."

NOTES

7. Herder, "Pell Grant Increase."
8. Stephen Burd, *Undermining Pell*, vol. 3 (New America, 2016), https://static.newamerica.org/attachments/12813-undermining-pell-volume-iii/Undermining-Pell-III-3.15bba9018bb54ad48f850f6f3a62a9fc.pdf.
9. Burd, *Undermining Pell*.
10. Burd, *Undermining Pell*.
11. Burd, *Undermining Pell*.
12. Burd, *Undermining Pell*.
13. Burd, *Undermining Pell*.
14. Burd, *Undermining Pell*.
15. Burd, *Undermining Pell*.
16. Burd, *Undermining Pell*.
17. Burd, *Undermining Pell*.
18. Opinion Editorial Board, "Helping Inmates Learn Behind Bars," *Washington Post*, August 26, 2025, https://www.washingtonpost.com/opinions/learning-behind-bars/2015/08/26/f28891c0-3c6e-11e5-b3ac-8a79bc44e5e2_story.html.
19. "Second Chance Pell Students Mark Progress for Prison Education," *Diverse Issues In Higher Education*, July 7, 2022, https://www.diverseeducation.com/students/article/15293991/graduation-of-miami-dade-college-second-chance-pell-students-marks-progress-for-prison-education.

CHAPTER 7: ADAM CLAYTON POWELL AND THE BLACK CHURCH

1. Wil Haygood, *King of the Cats: The Life and Times of Adam Clayton Powell, Jr.* (Houghton Mifflin, 1993).
2. Jamal Watson, "History of Helping: Black Churches Have Tradition of Giving College Scholarships," *Diverse Issues In Higher Education*, October 14, 2018, https://www.diverseeducation.com/institutions/hbcus/article/15103337/history-of-helping-black-churches-have-tradition-of-giving-college-scholarships.
3. Watson, "History of Helping."

4. Watson, "History of Helping."
5. Watson, "History of Helping."
6. Watson, "History of Helping."

CHAPTER 8: PILLARS OF SUPPORT

1. Associated Press, "Low Rawls, Singer and United Negro College Fund Champion, Dies at 72," *Daily Journal*, January 7, 2006, https://www.daily-journal.com/news/state/lou-rawls-singer-and-united-negro-college-fund-champion-dies-at-72/article_37ab2773-1529-5c14-8ee6-9c756e976fde.html.
2. William P. Barrett, "Turning 80, United Negro College Fund Stages a Revival," *Forbes*, December 12, 2023, https://www.forbes.com/sites/williampbarrett/2023/12/12/turning-80-united-negro-college-fund-stages-a-revival/.
3. "Transforming Futures: The Economic Engine of HBCUs," United Negro College Fund, n.d., https://uncf.org/programs/hbcu-impact.
4. "The Numbers Don't Lie: HBCUs Are Changing the College Landscape," United Negro College Fund, n.d., https://uncf.org/the-latest/the-numbers-dont-lie-hbcus-are-changing-the-college-landscape#:~:text=Though%20HBCUs%20make%20up%20only%20three%20percent%20of,produce%20almost%2020%25%20of%20all%20African%20American%20graduates.
5. "The Impact of HBCUs on Diversity in STEM Fields," United Negro College Fund, n.d., https://uncf.org/the-latest/the-impact-of-hbcus-on-diversity-in-stem-fields#:~:text=Twenty-five%20percent%20of%20African%20American%20graduates%20with%20STEM,engineering%20bachelor%E2%80%99s%20degrees%20to%20Black%20graduates%20from%202008-2012.

CHAPTER 9: THE COLLEGE FOR ALL ACT

1. US Senate Sergeant at Arms, "Sanders, Jayapal and Colleagues Introduce Legislation to Make College Tuition-Free and Debt-Free

for Working Families," press release, April 21, 2021, https://www.
sanders.senate.gov/press-releases/news-sanders-jayapal-and-
colleagues-introduce-legislation-to-make-college-tuition-free-and-
debt-free-for-working-families/.

2. Sarah Ewall-Wice, "Democrats Unveil Plan for Tuition-Free
College Amid Student Debt Crisis," *CBS News*, April 22, 2021,
https://www.cbsnews.com/news/student-loan-debt-free-college-
plan-bernie-sanders-pramila-jayapal/.

3. Briana Lopez, personal interview with the author, January
22, 2023.

RESOURCES AND
FURTHER READINGS

Akers, B., and M. M. Chingos. *Game of Loans: The Rhetoric and Reality of Student Debt*. Princeton University Press, 2016.

Avery, C., and S. Turner. "Student Loans: Do College Students Borrow Too Much—Or Not Enough?" *Journal of Economic Perspectives* 26, no. 1 (2012): 165–92.

Baker, D. J. "When Average Is Not Enough: A Case Study Examining the Variation in the Influences on Undergraduate Debt Burden." *AERA Open* 5, no. 2 (2019): 1–26.

Barr, A., and S. E. Turner. "A Letter and Encouragement: Does Information Increase Postsecondary Enrollment of UI Recipients?" *American Economic Journal: Economic Policy* 10, no. 3 (2018): 42–68.

Baum, S., and S. Schwartz. *How Much Debt Is Too Much? Defining Benchmarks for Manageable Student Debt*. College Board, 2006.

Best, J., and E. Best. *The Student Loan Mess: How Good Intentions Created a Trillion-Dollar Problem*. University of California Press, 2014.

Blagg, K. "Underwater on Student Debt: Understanding Consumer Credit and Student Loan Default." Urban Institute, August 2018.

Bleemer, Z., M. Brown, D. Lee, and W. Van der Klaauw. "Debt, Job Choice, and Financial Aid: Evidence from Law School Students." Federal Reserve Bank of New York *Staff Reports*, 2020.

Boatman, A., B. J. Evans, and A. Soliz. "Understanding Loan Aversion in Education: Evidence from High School Seniors, Community College Students, and Adults." *AERA Open* 3, no. 1 (2017): 1–16.

Cellini, S. R., and C. Goldin. "Does Federal Student Aid Raise Tuition? New Evidence on For-Profit Colleges." *American Economic Journal: Economic Policy* 6, no. 4 (2014): 174–206.

Chen, R., & M. Wiederspan. "Understanding the Determinants of Debt Burden Among College Graduates." *The Journal of Higher Education* 85, no. 4 (2014): 565–98.

Cheng, D., and J. Thompson. "Make It Simple, Keep It Fair: A Proposal to Streamline and Improve Income-Driven Repayment of Federal Student Loans." The Institute for College Access & Success, May 2017.

Chetty, R., J. N. Friedman, E. Saez, N. Turner, and D. Yagan. "Mobility Report Cards: The Role of Colleges in Intergenerational Mobility." Working Paper No. 23618. National Bureau of Economic Research, July 2017.

Collier, D. A. "The Impact of Student Loan Forgiveness Programs on Racial Wealth Gaps: A Critical Analysis." *Journal of Student Financial Aid* 49, no. 2 (2020): 1–14.

Cornelius, L. M., and S. A. Frank. "Student Loan Debt Levels and Their Implications for Borrowers, Society, and the Economy." *Educational Considerations* 42, no. 2 (2015): 35–38.

Deming, D. J., and C. R. Walters. "The Impact of Price Caps and Spending Cuts on U.S. Postsecondary Attainment." Working Paper No. 23736. National Bureau of Economic Research, August 2017.

Despard, M. R., D. Perantie, S. Taylor, M. Grinstein-Weiss, T. Friedline, and R. Raghavan. "Student Debt and Hardship: Evidence from a Large Sample of Low- and Moderate-Income Households." *Children and Youth Services Review* 70 (2016): 8–18.

Diverse Issues In Higher Education. "Study: Student Loan Debt Hinders Black Borrowers' Ability to Accumulate Wealth." *Diverse Issues In Higher Education*, 2021.

Doran, J. E., A. Kraha, L. R. Marks, E. J. Ameen, and N. H. El-Ghoroury. "Graduate Debt in Psychology: A Quantitative Analysis." *Training and Education in Professional Psychology* 10, no. 1 (2016): 3–13.

Dynarski, S. "An Economist's Perspective on Student Loans in the United States." Economic Studies Working Paper Series. Economic Studies at Brookings, September 2014.

Eaton, C., A. Goldstein, J. Habinek, M. Kumar, T. L. Stancyk, and G. Seashore Valletta. "Student Debt and the Transformation of Higher Education in the United States." *American Journal of Sociology* 127, no. 5 (2022): 1447–1503.

Elliott, W., and M. Lewis. "Student Debt Effects on Financial Well-Being: Research and Policy Implications." *Journal of Economic Surveys* 29, no. 4 (2015): 614–36.

Field, E. "Educational Debt Burden and Career Choice: Evidence from a Financial Aid Experiment at NYU Law School." *American Economic Journal: Applied Economics* 1, no. 1 (2009): 1–21.

Fos, V., A. Liberman, and C. Yannelis. "Debt and Human Capital: Evidence from Student Loans." *Journal of Financial Economics* 126, no. 3 (2017): 578–95.

Friedman, Z. "Student Loan Debt Statistics In 2019: A \$1.5 Trillion Crisis." *Forbes*, February 25, 2019.

Gicheva, D. "Student Loans or Marriage? A Look at the Highly Educated." *Economics of Education Review* 53 (2016): 207–16.

Goldrick-Rab, S. *Paying the Price: College Costs, Financial Aid, and the Betrayal of the American Dream.* University of Chicago Press, 2016.

Hanson, M. "Student Loan Debt Statistics." Education Data Initiative, 2021.

Herbst, D. "Liquidity and Insurance in Student Loan Contracts: The Effects of Income-Driven Repayment on Default and Consumption." Working Paper, 2020, https://drive.google.com/file/d/1A-gq_LIqffY6r2gDTcUK9-Y3ZV8Go6SU/view.

Hillman, N. W. "Borrowing and Repaying Student Loans." *Journal of Student Financial Aid* 45, no. 3 (2015): 35–48.

Houle, J. N., and C. Warner. "Into the Red and Back to the Nest? Student Debt, College Completion, and Returning to the Parental Home Among Young Adults." *Sociology of Education* 90, no. 1 (2017): 89–108.

Jackson, B. A., and J. R. Reynolds. "The Price of Opportunity: Race, Student Loan Debt, and College Achievement." *Sociological Inquiry* 83, no. 3 (2013): 335–68.

Johnson, A., T. Van Ostern, and A. White. "The Student Debt Crisis." Center for American Progress, October 25, 2012.

Kelchen, R. "An Empirical Examination of the Bennett Hypothesis in Law School Prices." *Economics of Education Review* 73 (2019): 101915.

Kim, J., and S. Chatterjee. "Student Loans, Health, and Life Satisfaction of US Households: Evidence from a Panel Study." *Journal of Family and Economic Issues* 40, no. 1 (2019): 36–50.

Kraiem, D. "The Cost of Opportunity: Student Debt and Social Mobility." *Suffolk University Law Review* 48 (2015): 689–750.

Krishnan, K., and P. Wang. "The Cost of Financing Education: Can Student Debt Hinder Entrepreneurship?" *Management Science* 65, no. 10 (2019): 4522–54.

Lochner, L., and A. Monge-Naranjo. "Student Loans and Repayment: Theory, Evidence, and Policy." *Handbook of the Economics of Education* 5 (2016): 397–478.

Looney, A., and C. Yannelis. "How Useful Are Default Rates? Borrowers with Large Balances and Student Loan Repayment." *Economics of Education Review* 71 (2019): 135–45.

Lucca, D. O., T. Nadauld, and K. Shen. "Credit Supply and the Rise in College Tuition: Evidence from the Expansion in Federal Student Aid Programs." *The Review of Financial Studies* 32, no. 2 (2019): 423–66.

Ma, J., M. Pender, and M. Welch. *Education Pays 2019: The Benefits of Higher Education for Individuals and Society*. College Board, 2019.

Marx, B. M., and L. J. Turner. "Student Loan Nudges: Experimental Evidence on Borrowing and Educational Attainment." *American Economic Journal: Economic Policy* 11, no. 2 (2019): 108–41.

Mezza, A., D. Ringo, S. Sherlund, and K. Sommer. "Student Loans and Homeownership." *Journal of Labor Economics* 38, no. 1 (2020): 215–60.

Mueller, H. M., and C. Yannelis. "The Rise in Student Loan Defaults." *Journal of Financial Economics* 131, no. 1 (2019): 1–19.

Mulhern, C. "Beyond Teachers: Estimating Individual Guidance Counselors' Effects on Educational Attainment." Working Paper, 2019, https://cepr.harvard.edu/files/cepr/files/counselors_mulhern.pdf.

Page, L. C., and J. Scott-Clayton. "Improving College Access in the United States: Barriers and Policy Responses." *Economics of Education Review* 51 (2016): 4–22.

Perna, L. W., J. Kvaal, and R. Ruiz. "Understanding Student Debt: Implications for Federal Policy and Future Research." *The Annals of the American Academy of Political and Social Science* 671, no. 1 (2017): 270–86.

Quadlin, N. Y., and D. Rudel. "Responsibility or Liability? Student Loan Debt and Time Use in College." *Social Forces* 94, no. 2 (2015): 589–614.

Rothstein, J., and C. E. Rouse. "Constrained After College: Student Loans and Early-Career Occupational Choices." *Journal of Public Economics* 95, nos. 1–2 (2011): 149–63.

Scott-Clayton, J. "The Looming Student Loan Default Crisis Is Worse Than We Thought." *Brookings Institution Evidence Speaks Reports* 2, no. 34 (2018).

Seamster, L., and R. Charron-Chénier. "Predatory Inclusion and Education Debt: Rethinking the Racial Wealth Gap." *Social Currents* 4, no. 3 (2017): 199–207.

Sieg, H., and Y. Wang. "The Impact of Student Debt on Education, Career, and Marriage Choices of Female Lawyers." *European Economic Review* 109 (2018): 124–47.

St. Amour, M. "What Happens Before College Matters." Inside Higher Ed, October 19, 2020.

Stolper, H. "Student Debt and the Siren Song of For-Profit Colleges." *Quarterly Journal of Economics* 133, no. 2 (2018): 888–932.

Supiano, B. "What Does Student-Loan Forgiveness Mean for College Costs?" The Chronicle of Higher Education, 2022.

Tatham, M. "Student Loan Debt Climbs to $1.4 Trillion in 2019." Experian, December 21, 2019.

Taylor, Z. W., and I. Bicak. "What Is the FAFSA? An Adult Learner Knowledge Survey of Student Financial Aid Jargon." *Journal of Adult and Continuing Education* 25, no. 1 (2019): 94–112.

Whitsett, H. C. "High Debt, Low Information: A Survey of Student Loan Borrowers." NERA Economic Consulting, 2018.

Woo, J. H., and L. Horn. "Reaching the Limit: Undergraduates Who Borrow the Maximum Amount in Federal Direct Loans: 2011–12." Stats in Brief. NCES 2016–408. National Center for Education Statistics, 2016.

Zhan, M., X. Xiang, and W. Elliott. "Education Loans and Wealth Building Among Young Adults." *Children and Youth Services Review* 66 (2016): 67–75.

Zhang, L. "Effects of College Educational Debt on Graduate School Attendance and Early Career and Lifestyle Choices." *Education Economics* 21, no. 2 (2013): 154–75.

ABOUT THE AUTHOR

Jamal Watson is the executive editor of *Diverse: Issues In Higher Education*. He is also a professor of communications and associate dean at Trinity Washington University, located in Washington, DC. Watson earned a bachelor's degree from Georgetown University, a master's degree from the Graduate School of Journalism at Columbia University, a master's degree in higher education from the University of Delaware, and a master's degree and PhD in Afro-American studies from the University of Massachusetts, Amherst.

Diverse: Issues In Higher Education is the preeminent source of critical news, information, and insightful commentary on the full range of issues concerning diversity in American higher education. *Diverse* began writing about diversity, equity, and inclusion in higher education long before diversity and multiculturalism became "hot-button" issues. Today, our mission remains as true as it was more than forty years ago: to provide information that is honest, thorough, and balanced. We seek, through traditional and nontraditional mediums, to be change agents and generate public policies that resolve inequities that still exist today. In fulfilling our mission, we believe we are helping to build the educational, cultural, social, and economic structures necessary to allow every individual to reach their full potential and thus contribute to the greater good of their community and the nation.

With more than forty years of experience covering education, *Diverse* is the only biweekly newsmagazine focusing on matters of access, diversity, inclusion, and opportunity for all in higher education. Its unparalleled coverage of issues surrounding topics such as tenure, salary, faculty, students, recruitment, retention, access, and equity earned *Diverse* the 2002 Folio Award for best education publication in America. And as our communities have grown more diverse, so, too, has our editorial focus.

Launched in 1984 as *Black Issues In Higher Education*, the magazine focused on the role of and issues pertaining to African Americans in higher education. To better reflect inclusivity and America's changing demographics, in 2005 we renamed the magazine *Diverse: Issues In Higher Education* and expanded coverage to address issues that affect Asian Americans, Hispanics/Latinos, Native American Indians, people with disabilities, seniors, LGBTQIA people, veterans, and other underrepresented groups in higher education. Our companion website translates our flagship brand, *Diverse*, into a digital medium so advertisers can extend their print messages online and engage and interact with the *Diverse* audience. Through our signature events, the Dr. John Hope Franklin Awards and the Arthur Ashe Jr. Sports Scholar Awards, sponsors can interface with scholars, researchers, faculty, administrators, and business leaders from across the country.